THE POLITICS OF URBANISM

The New Federalism WITHDRAWN

★

★

★

GEORGE C. S. BENSON, Professor and President
Emeritus
Director of Henry Salvatori
Center
Claremont Men's College
Claremont, California

Politics in Government Series
Mary Earhart Dillon, Editor

BARRON'S EDUCATIONAL

SERIES, INC.

WOODBURY, NEW YORK

All inquiries should be addressed to:
Barron's Educational Series, Inc.
113 Crossways Park Drive
Woodbury, New York 11797

Library of Congress Catalog Card No. 70–189864
International Standard Book No. 0–8120–0445–0

PRINTED IN THE UNITED STATES OF AMERICA

PREFACE ★

In 1931, I taught my first class in Municipal Government at Harvard University; in 1941, *The New Centralization,* containing all too brief comments on local governmental units, was published; in 1955, appeared the *Report* of the United States Commission on Intergovernmental Relations, for which I had served as Research Director. I returned to the study of urban problems with an increased sense that "intergovernmental relations" is a vital issue and with pleasure to find a growing interest in this field among younger scholars.

Certain changes in outlook are noticeable during recent years. Formerly, the prevailing idea among "liberal" professors (that is, over 90% of those writing on these topics) was: "Anything the states and cities can do, the federal government can do better." Omniscience, even clairvoyance, was presumably centered in Washington. This was the era of the innumerable special grants—devised by the "best experts" in federal departments and all too frequently not well geared into the machinery of other levels of government. Not too curiously, ideological extremes meshed in opposition to effective cooperation in a truly federal pattern. Some advocates of state and local autonomy were so averse to *any* federal intervention that they also argued against block grants or shared revenues.

Happily by 1971 the situation has changed markedly. If there is less confidence that Washington knows best about Jonesville, there is also less insistence that Jonesville should remain an insulated unit. In other words, more people are realizing that a successful inter-relation of federal, state, county, metropolitan, and urban levels must, however complex the problem, be worked out.

I feel strongly that both national and state governments have failed to realize that they are dealing, by direct grants or otherwise, with governmental *units;* that innumerable uncoordinated grants have a chaotic effect on local administration; that often conflicting federal and state policies tend to divide communities; and that there is a urgent need to re-think federal-state, federal-urban, state-urban, urban-suburban relations. My knowledge is limited and my suggestions are tentative.

My acknowledgements extend to a very large number of the people who have written on urban and intergovernmental problems during the past forty years. I wish that I might say "to all" who have written, but I confess that my reading has not been as inclusive as I could have desired. This study has been prepared in "off-duty" time, and neither my recent employer, the Department of Defense, nor my past and future employer, Claremont Men's College, have any responsibility for any of the content.

I would like to express a special appreciation to the Henry Salvatori Center for the study of individual freedom in the modern world.

GEORGE C. S. BENSON
Claremont Men's College

CONTENTS ★

Contents

TITLES IN THIS SERIES

PUBLISHED

General Editor: Mary Earhart Dillon, formerly Chairman of the Department of Political Science, Queens College of the City University of New York

INTRODUCTION ★

The Politics of Government Series is a continuing publication of paperbacks by distinguished scholars on controversial political and social issues of "here and now." These pamphlets provide students of current American problems with ready and valid technical aid as source material for discussions, reports, term papers, speeches, and debates. Invaluable are the 100 appropriate topics in each pamphlet from which the student may more easily prepare his class assignment, and also a recent bibliography.

The Politics of Urbanism: The New Federalism by George C. S. Benson discusses the problem of the decadence of the cities and the complicated cause. While some mayors talk of such easy solutions as ending the war in Vietnam and the diversion of billions in federal funds to their use, scholars in urbanism discount such measures as only a partial remedy since there would still have been the decline of the cities without the war. With sharp insight, the author analyzes the staggering urban problems which have been developing for decades, but he points especially to the alienation of people. He sees hope for the future and the gradual revitalizing of the cities as creative centers of society again and gives a blue-print for this achievement.

Professor Benson is a well-known scholar in the field of intergovernmental relations. He was Research Director of the Council of State Governments (Chicago), Director of Administration in the Office for Price Administration (Washington), and Research Director for the Commission on Intergovernmental Relations (Washington). With a rare combination of experience in public service and brilliant scholarship, Professor Benson has achieved wide recognition in the field of political science as teacher, administrator, author, and college president. Graduating from Pomona College cum laude, he took his Ph.D. at Harvard University and began his teaching career there. Later he taught at the University of Chicago, University of Michigan, and Northwestern University. He was president of Claremont Men's College (California) from 1946 to 1969. Currently he is on leave to serve in Washington as Deputy Assistant Secretary of Defense (Education). He has published articles and several books, the most famous of which was the *New Centralization*.

THE PLIGHT
OF THE CITIES

★
★
★

Accepted facts" are often accepted rather uncritically. For instance, it is "well-known" that ghetto life is a dead end. Currently, this is probably so—especially for the blacks. However, by any possible collection of statistics, cities in the United States have until quite recently provided one of the greatest upward-mobility opportunities for the poorer classes. From the ghetto, inhabited at various times by Irish, Jews, Orientals, Eastern Europeans, and others, have come financiers, administrators, scientists, humanistic scholars, technical experts, poets, artists, and some of the best of our political leaders. For generations, urban America has truly been a Land of Promise. Even those who did not achieve success in any field felt little bitterness because they had visible evidence that success was possible, and that the American city provided more opportunity than the situations from which they had migrated. There has, of course, also been a vast influx of rural Americans seeking broader fields of advancement. In 1789, 95% of the population was rural. In 1960, 70% of the population was urban. In 1971, the urban proportion was probably larger.

It would seem profitable at this point, before discussing the "urban problem," to make a clear distinction between the central city and the metropolitan area. Suburbs are currently the fastest growing aspect of America. They include, in terms of residence, over half the population of metropolitan areas, yet, at least thus far, they do not suffer most of the evils found in the central cities.

While, for this reason, we must often consider the "central city" separately from the metropolitan area, we must always bear in mind the inescapable fact that there is no solution to the central city problems which will not affect the larger area. "Town and country" are as inter-related today as they were in the original New England townships.

1

There is no question that some of our major cities are losing ground in various ways: in physical appearance, in public services, in law and order, and, above all, in opportunities for their poorer citizens. This chapter will discuss some of the urgent problems to be faced. The next chapter considers the underlying difficulties. Possible solutions will be analyzed in later chapters.

The Physical Environment

This is no place to discuss Medieval Guilds or egocentric Princes, but most large American cities would have benefited aesthetically from either or both. Tastes vary, and those who admire the best of eighteenth century architecture may not admire the best of mid-twentieth century architecture, but clearly there is very little of either in American cities. Most "downtowns" are dreary examples of the worst of the functional combined with the worst of the over-ornamented. Moreover, streets are filled with noisy vehicles. Air is polluted by auto exhaust, emissions from furnaces of office and apartment buildings, and often by waste gases from nearby industrial operations.

The business district is not aesthetically pleasing (except inside tastefully furnished offices), but the sections circling it where poorer people work and live are even more depressing. There are apartment blocks in New York City or Chicago which are not usually classified as slums, but which nevertheless are sorry places in which to house citizens of the world's wealthiest nation. We have all seen the garbage and trash in the alleys, the pathetic absence of shrubbery or grass, the dirty or broken windows, the proximity of the drab factory to dingy apartment buildings. This type of property can, and frequently does, degenerate into the unbelievable squalor of the true slum—breeder of illness, poverty, and crime. In our major cities, from a third to a half of non-white housing units are classified as deteriorating or dilapidated.[1]

There are exceptions, of course. Some parts of Manhattan are attractive. Almost all cities have pleasant suburbs, and many have respectable, sometimes "luxury," residential areas immediately adjacent to the central city. A few, like Los Angeles and Detroit, were developed in the motor age and are ringed by many square miles of modest but attractive one-family residences with gardens. Even these latter, however, are constantly subject to the danger of becoming "run-down" if even a few tenants or owners neglect the property.

No one disputes the fact that practically all of our cities contain areas of which they are ashamed. The error of most zealous reformers is that they fail to realize how complex is the problem of improvement. Any "program" becomes a tangle of political, financial, legal, economic, and personal factors. Strict enforcement of building maintenance laws, for example, has often become a political issue. All too frequently, an entrenched "machine" or bureau, immune to opposition, while theoretically not opposed to law enforcement, is, for various reasons, not particularly interested in it. While unquestionably some unscrupulous owners of slum property fight such laws in order to increase profits, it is also true that some owners genuinely cannot afford to maintain the buildings properly. There are areas in which tenement dwellings have been abandoned by owners who found it financially impossible to pay taxes, insurance, and up-keep costs out of rent receipts, let alone make interest on their investment. Obsolete downtown buildings should be renovated or replaced by their owners, but, except in a few fortunate cities, these individuals hesitate to risk new capital in an area which is already heavily taxed and may perhaps show signs of irreversible decline. Slum areas have sometimes been replaced by federal (and a very little state) public housing. Experience shows that public housing units sometimes deteriorate very rapidly.

Obviously something should and can be done, but there is no simplistic solution to a problem which is inherently complex.

Getting To Work And Home

The problems of transportation are midway between the problems of physical aspect and the problems of public services, and they at times spill over into the problems of sociology.

Even the relatively prosperous face the daily task of trying to get to work, mostly by autos, in downtown cities which were clearly not designed for the morning inflow or evening outflow of cars. The trip, both ways, is crowded, polluted, tiresome, and time-consuming. Once the workers arrive, there is the problem of parking. Parking in lots or in buildings is expensive. However, it might be noted that an estimate has been made of the "investment cost" *per parking space* in a downtown parking building in one large metropolitan area. It was $12,000.00. Obviously, anyone investing that much money expects some profit.

Buses and subways as they now exist are a partial solution, but only partial. After the Watts riots in Los Angeles, it was discovered that many Watts residents who could not afford a car simply could not find public transportation from their area to places of possible work.

If and when the cities can afford them, better methods of transportation may develop. The San Francisco Bay area is finishing a rapid transit system of 65 miles, featuring automatic fare collection and completely computerized train controls. Southern California Rapid Transit is working on a diesel exhaust emission control system which will reduce the air pollution element of the existing buses. The Los Angeles Department of Airports is studying a 16 mile line of 150-miles-per-hour tracked air cushion vehicles. Columbia, Maryland, is planning an automated system of carrying passengers around the city. New York City hopes to air-condition its 70-year-old IRT subway line.

These are challenging examples. But cities face great financial and legal problems. Right-of-way may involve both money and the law; certainly construction costs of rapid transit systems are staggering to cities which cannot meet their current fiscal burdens.

Law Enforcement

Our large cities are now being filled with the poor and the ill-educated. Obviously such people require more public services if they are to be protected, to be cared for, to be prepared to take a place in a sharply competitive society. Per capita costs for law enforcement, for welfare, for schooling, for health services are greater in urban areas. This section concentrates on one of the greatest problems—control of crime. The extent of crime in recent years in the United States is shocking. In 1969, reported crime included 14,500 murders; 306,-000 aggravated assaults; 36,000 forcible rapes; and at least 300,-000 robberies. Many more went unreported. Crime, of course, is not an exclusively urban phenomenon, but it should be noted that in cities over 250,000 over-all crime rates were 100% greater than in suburban areas. Violent crime rates were 3 to 8 times greater. In Washington, D.C. in 1970, violent crime ran almost 10 times as great per capita as in the surrounding suburbs.[2] Later we shall consider more fully the effect of other aspects of slum life on youth, but here we shall merely note that in 1961, 14% of all urban persons arrested for aggravated assault were under 18 years of age. Non-urban arrests for the same offense included only 9% under 18.

It has been maintained that the statistics which show that arrest rates for non-whites and under-eighteens is nearly two and a half times the average for the general population, have been distorted because non-whites and the young are more likely to be "busted" by unsympathetic police. But the other side of this picture is that blacks are also the special *victims* of crime. They constitute only 12% of the total population, and only 20% of the national average of central city population. Nevertheless, a seventeen-city survey found that blacks were 70% of homicide victims, 60% of rape victims, and 40% of robbery victims. Personal violence in the inner cities is not racially oriented.

There are many tentative sociological explanations, and sometimes they are inconsistent. For instance, Durkheim, a French sociologist of the early twentieth century, discussed "anomie" (the sense that the individual was not part of any social group). This feeling of anonymity in a large city could explain a drifting semi-criminal element which felt immune because of public apathy. We all remember the story of Kitty Genovese, who was slowly stabbed to death in an area where hundreds heard her screams but no one bothered either to help her or even to call the police. On the other hand, there is the sociological theory of cohesive groups which function *as* cohesive groups, but always on the periphery of what they consider the "Established Order." These people have no feeling of "anomie": they "belong," and "belonging" is important. When families are crowded together in slums, it becomes hard for parents to maintain control. Boys drift off into gangs; girls become camp followers. *Every* ethnic group which has gone through certain slum areas has had a higher crime rate until the people were able to move out of the area.[3]

Professor Banfield, in his thoughtful book *The Unheavenly City,* suggests that the large concentration of young males in the cities, far greater, for example, than in the depression decade, has markedly affected the crime rate for various reasons. Desirable as minimum wage laws may be in intent, they do keep semi-educated and totally unskilled youths from securing employment. These young men, poor in the midst of general American affluence and "present" rather than "future" oriented, tend to take illegally what they cannot earn. (And it should be noted that careless people who leave ignition keys in cars or fail to lock office or apartment doors provide temptation to many youths who would hesitate at more violent crimes.) Of course, the increasing use of drugs among the young is an important factor. It has been estimated that someone thoroughly addicted to such hard drugs as heroin needs from $50 to $80 a day to satisfy his needs. Clearly this is an amount of money not available even to an employed young man.

Even though the total expenditures for policing in urban areas are steadily increasing, and though as cities grow in size, they employ a larger number of police per 10,000 inhabitants, the results have not been encouraging. It may be, as we shall discuss shortly, that some of the problem arises from mutual suspicion between police and black urban dwellers; but it is clear that increased police forces alone have not solved the problem of controlling crime.

In addition to a steadily rising rate of ordinary crimes, our cities have had in the summers of 1964, 1965, 1966, and especially 1967 and 1968, a series of major riots—most of which had at least some aspects of black antagonism to the "white establishment." (There have been riots since 1968, but smaller in number and less extensive.) Yet, as in the case of other ghetto crimes, the chief victims have been blacks. There has been extensive destruction of black housing and of stores serving black patrons, and in some areas the damage has not yet been repaired.

There have been quite divergent explanations for the riots— probably for the excellent reason that most of them have arisen from a very complex variety of causes working together to reach a point of explosion.

Banfield is inclined to think that recent riots in American cities stem more from the presence of many more-or-less "foot-loose" young males in the central cities than from a basically racist factor. He cites the many riots which have occurred during other periods in both American and non-American cities, including the New York Draft riots in 1863. Moreover, it is his opinion that, in absolute terms of the amount of property destroyed or people injured or killed, riots are not of major importance in the crime records. The title of his chapter is roughly indicative of his view: "Rioting Mainly for Fun and Profit."[4]

Quite different is the conclusion of the National Advisory Commission on Civil Disorders, appointed by President Johnson in 1967 and chaired by Otto Kerner, then Governor of Illinois. This Commission believes that the riots were primarily black protests against white racism. Its recommendations ranged from better police and National Guard techniques to comprehensive social reform programs including ampler welfare, more public housing, and more school integration.

There are probably elements of accuracy in both analyses. Since the Kerner Commission represents current sociological opinion, its recommendations are more likely to be implemented. It is doubtful if the results achieved will match the hopes of the Commission, but they may help to make a better society. One thing seems clear. In many cities, there *does* exist tension between police and black citizens—a tension exag-

gerated at times of riot. While the writer thinks it is simplistic
to divide people into good guys and bad guys, and suspects that
there are faults on both sides, it is obviously to the advantage of
all urbanites to promote the feeling that the police are the protec-
tors of black as well as white.

Poverty and Welfare

Of course not all poverty is localized in large cities, perhaps
about a third of it, if we take over-all national statistics. However,
the problem is very substantial in urban areas. For instance,
New York City which has less than half of the total population
of New York State included almost 80% of the state's welfare
recipients in 1968. Baltimore and Chicago had similar propor-
tions in relation to their states.[5] Moreover, poverty in the central
cities presents two difficult complicating factors: race and intergovernmental relations.

The Kerner Commission reported that in 1964, 41.7% of non-
whites below the poverty level lived in the urban core areas, in
contrast to only 23.8% of poor whites. Almost a third of city-
dwelling non-white families of two or more members lived in
poverty, whereas the comparable figure for whites was 8.8%.
Poverty was more than twice as prevalent among non-white
families headed by females as among those headed by males.
Since in central cities 26% of all non-white families of two or
more persons had female "head of household" status (in contrast
to 12% among white families) this 100% differential gains added
racial significance.[6] Not only, then, is the current concentration
of poor blacks and other non-whites in large cities a present
problem; since discrimination limits the upward mobility of
these groups out of the slums, they tend to develop an almost
hopeless poverty syndrome which immensely increases other
problems of health, crime, disorder, and to some extent education.

The fact that costs of welfare are financed by various levels of
government further complicates the picture. The federal government assumes a share, as do practically all of the states. In some

states the county is the local unit of administration, but in others it is the city. In either case, federal and state governments usually determine the amount to be spent by the local unit, often without adequate consideration of the actual fiscal situation of the latter.

Education

In previous decades, the various ethnic groups who have lived in the poorer sections of our central cities have found the public schools to be the key to economic, social, and intellectual advancement. Today, however, there is some evidence that this is no longer so—even though educational systems constitute the largest item in local governmental expenditure. What Former Commissioner of Education Francis Keppel said about the New York situation could well be applied to many others: "[Urban specialists say] Public schools, once the chief instrument for social, economic, and political mobility are now a chief instrument for blocking Negroes with other minority group children." The New York City School System, which once ranked at the summit of American public education, is caught in a spiral of decline. The true measure of a structure of formal education is its effect on individual children. By this standard, the system of public education is failing because vast numbers are not learning adequately. The city, as a whole, is paying a very heavy price for the decline.[7]

In a major study of "Equality of Educational Opportunity," James S. Coleman and associates concluded that the average minority pupil (except Oriental-Americans) scored lower on tests at every level than the average white student.[8] Moreover, as the two groups moved from first to twelfth grade, the differential in scores increased. These differences appeared in city and county schools, in the north and in the south. However, it should be noted that the twelfth grade Negro in the non-metropolitan south was behind the twelfth grade Negro in the metropolitan northeast—some indication that the northeastern urban schools did provide some advantages.

The question of why our city schools are failing with these minority groups is of vital importance when we consider that the black family is usually confined to living in the central city because of suburban prejudices. These children must be properly educated in urban schools if they are to be properly educated at all.

Various answers have been suggested. Mrs. Annie Stein, long an administrator in the New York City school system, asserts that deliberate racism has been practiced by New York School Board leaders, by administrators, by at least some teachers, and, at times, by the Teachers Union in an effort to keep blacks and Puerto Ricans in the lowest stratum by calculated indifference to improved methods of teaching.[9] John J. Theobald, Executive Vice President of the New York Institute of Technology, and former New York educational and municipal executive, believes that New York schools have conscientiously tried out various experiments for helping minority groups and faults them only for failure to stay with, expand, or improve on the experiments.[10] A third viewpoint divides the "guilt." Public schools in slum areas present a difficult problem for administrators. It is still a subject of argument as to whether schools are not cooperating with their clients or their clients are not cooperating with the schools.[11]

On the basis of reading and peripheral professional experience, the writer ventures a few generalizations. Our city schools are not helping the present residents of slum areas to move forward as they have helped earlier residents. Perhaps part of the problem is that we are now attempting to educate *all* of the children instead of, as in the past, only the brighter and more highly motivated ones. Perhaps it is that many previous ethnic groups, while desperately poor, had a heritage which respected and encouraged intellectual achievement. Perhaps it is that these earlier ethnic groups had tangible evidence that academic excellence or at least the acquisition of special skills did provide opportunity for upward mobility, whereas American blacks especially have had their incentives dulled by the feeling that the upper strata were closed to them no matter what they did.

In any event, any school system which is dealing with a group which harbors a feeling of discriminatory treatment must make herculean *and* imaginative efforts to combine two approaches. A respectful attitude both to individual students and to their cultural background is essential. Equally essential is the desire and the ability to convey to a student that he need not disavow his own cultural heritage in order to fit into the requirements of upward mobility in American society. This is perhaps the greatest challenge ever faced by our school teachers, administrators, and educational advisors.

The "People" and the City

It seems to the writer that there are two distinct problems— what might be called psychological problems—facing the city-dweller of today: one is confined to the under-privileged minority groups; the other includes a very large number of people holding reasonably decent middle-level jobs who are definitely outside of the slum category.

We have already noted that, in general, earlier immigrants have not only graduated from the slums into better residential areas and better employment, but that many have been brilliantly successful. The myth of WASP-controlled America *is* a myth. For instance, Jews of German and Russian origin and Orientals are passing, educationally and economically, the original "old American" stock as well as British, German, Irish, and Scotch families. The two main exceptions are the so-called "Spanish surname" group (Puerto Ricans in the east, Mexican-Americans in the mid, south, and far west) and the black Americans. It may be true to some extent that certain aspects of "Gringo" culture are distasteful to people of Latin culture, and the recent upsurge of interest in African culture indicates that blacks also desire to retain some distinctive characteristics. This is laudable. The United States as a whole would be enriched by the preservation of various ethnic contributions. But neither the blacks and browns, nor the country, are benefitted by a system which encourages "ghetto psychology"—a feeling of helplessness engendered by a sense of being hopelessly trapped in an atmosphere of poor housing, poor education, high crime rate, and job discrimination. (It should be added that job discrimination is not only on the part of employers; white-controlled unions have always been as guilty and at the present time are probably more so.) The problem becomes circular. Massed together without contacts among the better educated and economically more advanced citizens, ill-prepared for a competitive society, often the victims of poor city politics, these people increase the problems of welfare, education, and law enforcement, while the area which they inhabit loses the tax resources necessary to support such services.

Even those who live above the slum level may suffer from *anomie*—the sense of *not belonging* discussed earlier. They occupy miles of often dingy apartment houses, owned by men they have never met. They work for large and impersonal corporations or governmental departments. They shop at stores where no one recognizes them. They have no feeling of involvement, either at work or at home. Certainly there have been efforts to overcome this sense of "lostness." Churches, unions, and other voluntary associations have tried. Moreover, many progressive business leaders have organized sports clubs, recreational groups, office parties, even participatory management with a view to filling the void. But city governments with rare exceptions have made no comparable efforts. Millions of city-dwellers do not in any real sense feel that they are "citizens."

Conclusion

Banfield, in *The Unheavenly City,* makes a more detached analysis of the urban crisis than do most writers. He points out that suburban and some central city dwellers live better than ever before, and that such problems as welfare and poor education are even more prevalent in many rural areas. The admitted loss of value in big city down-town properties is merely comparable to other economic results of changing values. A city is bankrupt because it cannot or will not levy taxes to support the services it needs, and, in turn, our concept of necessary standards has risen above the capacity of many cities to maintain.

All of these points are legitimate. Nevertheless, there is undoubtedly more of an urban crisis than Banfield will admit. Fortunately, not many cities present as grim a picture as Newark. Mayor Kenneth A. Gibson provided before a Congressional hearing the following appalling statistics about his city: 11% unemployed; 30% on relief; the highest per capita crime, venereal disease and infant mortality rates in the nation; one of the highest real estate taxes ($844 on a house assessed at $10,000); 60% of its land area tax exempt and an anticipated deficit of 43% of the operating budget.

This is, of course, an extreme case, but there is definite evidence that several of our central cities are actually going downhill in terms of educational opportunities and law enforcement. Perhaps not all parts of the country can rise equally fast, but in a nation as wealthy as ours, every segment should be moving up. And our cities, the most visible aspect of American life, mecca for travellers, and final goal of most newly arrived immigrants as well as many rural Americans, should at least approximate the national average.

The following chapters will discuss the reasons for the urban problem, the division of functions between levels of government, and the possibilities of help from various other levels of government. The final chapter will review the New Federalism, dealing mostly with the Nixon administration but to some extent with the Johnson period, and the effect of all the changes mentioned on the main functions of urban government.

UNDERLYING PROBLEMS $\mathcal{2}$ ★ ★ ★

$\mathbf{B}$efore one can possibly discuss the improvement of relations between federal, state, and local levels of government in solution of the urban problem, some consideration must be given to the enormous existing complexity of "local" government.

The Metropolitan Area

American cities have developed in varying ways. San Francisco, Philadelphia, and Boston have grown slowly. Los Angeles and Detroit, both associated with the auto age, expanded rapidly. All have faced the problem of widening boundaries, and all have faced the problem of adjacent settlements which became, in fact, part of the metropolitan area. Local government is now a melange of municipal government, county government, and special districts. The situation is further confused by the fact that legal authority over both counties and cities is vested in the state government which may set limits on local taxing or borrowing, consolidate or abolish local units, and in general specify all operational details. Until recently, most state governments have not shown great wisdom in their supervision of urban affairs.

A few examples may be helpful in understanding why there have been frequent references to the "mess" of local government.

The city of St. Louis, which is its own county, includes only a little more than a third of the population of its metropolitan area. More than 100 other municipalities, all in practice dependent and all legally autonomous, surround it. Seven counties and two states are properly within its metropolitan area. Cook County is by no means synonymous with Chicago; 119 other independent municipalities are within its borders. Eleven other metropolitan areas in the country each contain more than 50 municipalities. San Francisco, which is its own county, now finds itself frozen on the end of a peninsula while its real population is 300% elsewhere. The city of Los Angeles was a tremendously cohesive factor in the early growth of Southern California because it was a source of water—a rare commodity in that semi-arid region. However, the formation of a Metropolitan Water District in the 1930's permitted suburbanization in the Los Angeles area. New York City, which achieved most of its growth prior to 1918, managed to incorporate several counties (now boroughs) into its municipal area, but it now faces problems which spill over even these expanded political boundaries.

This often chaotic multiplication of political sub-divisions brings obvious difficulties. Law enforcement agencies must pursue criminals through unrelated jurisdictions. Fire-fighting forces need to work out intricate cooperative plans. Streets, sewers, and zoning face arbitrary boundaries bearing no relation to the physical situations. In many states, the county administers at least some welfare and public health services within the city limits and, in non-incorporated areas, other normally municipal functions. Moreover, any effort at rationalization is impeded by the fact that state *constitutions* often carefully prescribe the election and duties of county officials.

One of the worst difficulties caused by the governmental fragmentation of the metropolitan area is the fence it places around the central city blacks. Their chance of moving from ghetto to suburbs, as other ethnic groups have done before them, is severely limited by prejudices, zoning laws, and other restrictions applied by suburbs.

The financial condition of the central cities is a serious obstacle to solving many of the evils of metropolitan areas. Once viewed as the financial strongholds within the states, these units are now in fiscal difficulties. Much of the land area is depreciating as a tax base. Moreover, average family income in cities is steadily declining in comparison with that in the suburbs. In 1960, the city average was $5,940; the suburban average, $6,707. By 1967, the figures were $7,813 and $9,637.[1] Obviously, expenditures for welfare, for police, and especially for education should be greater in disadvantaged areas, whether black, brown, or white. After the Watts riots of 1965, Max Rafferty, then California Superintendent of Schools, correctly commented that

much of the difficulty arose from the fact that far more money
was spent per capita on the education of Beverly Hills children
than on Watts children, while the ratios should have been reversed. The simple explanation is that suburbs spend more on
education because they can afford to do so.[2] Conversely, the welfare, police, and health burdens of the central cities are far
greater, and accordingly these must spend more on non-educa-
tional functions than is necessary in the suburbs. In 1964, the
former spent $232 per capita on non-educational functions as
compared to $132 per capita in the latter.

An immeasurable but very substantial loss from the fraction-
alization of metropolitan areas is the fact that persons of education and wealth who might help lead the city government to
better efforts, frequently live outside the city. They may participate in some "down-town" charitable as well as business and
social activities, but their legal residence keeps them out of the
central city's political life. Few can doubt that Chicago politics
would be on a higher plane if the North Shore villages were part
of the city of Chicago. Boston's politics might be immensely different if the Newtons and Brookline were part of the city.

Special Districts

Perhaps some of the greatest confusion is introduced into the
local governmental picture by the multiplicity of special districts. Often not included in the category, but certainly of major
importance, are the school districts which are totally autonomous from other units of local government. Members of the
school board are usually directly elected; they determine school
tax rates, general educational policy, and plant development;
and they select the educational executive. In most jurisdictions,
the school tax is larger than the city or county tax, but it is
determined by a group independent of responsibility to, or even
anything but purely voluntary cooperation with, other local
units. A United States Commissioner of Education has ques-
tioned the wisdom of such total separation and has commented:
"The schools are going to have to seek the partnership and the

active collaboration of the programs in the city which provide housing, health, welfare, recreational and family services."[3] According to Bollens, school districts have been decreasing in number as a result of state legislation financially supporting consolidation of school districts, but the number of other special districts continues to rise. In his monumental study of these local governmental units created for a "special purpose" under provisions of permissive state law, he notes that as of 1961, there were 79,000 of them "constituting about two-thirds of the approximately 116,000 governmental units in the United States."[4]

To the political theorist, wistfully seeking a simple structure of local government readily responsive to the public, these special districts, which range in function from mosquito abatement in New Jersey to large scale irrigation in the southwest, are particularly repugnant. However, as in many other aspects of government, there are pros as well as cons.

It is certainly true that special districts contribute to a lack of over-all responsibility for urban problems. Bollens found an average of 96 governments per metropolitan area.[5] Directors of the districts are sometimes elected, sometimes appointed by the governor, sometimes chosen by the governments of member cities. Districts often have the power to float bonds or to tax—frequently with no regard to the bond issues or taxes of the other local governments which overlap the districts. Thus a property owner in a particular area may find himself paying several kinds of taxes to several different local units. Sometimes the districts are so unresponsive to popular will that one California student entitled his study: "Special Districts or Special Dynasties?"

Why, then, does the number continue to increase? Bollens offers several reasons.

First, the existing units of government may be unsuitable. For instance, a number of cities may be interested in water supply or sewage disposal, but none is large enough alone to swing a practicable project. If these cities are located in more than one county, or if the one county within which they exist is hamstrung by state provisions rigidly regulating county administration and county functions, a new district is the only alternative. It must be remembered that legal governmental units rarely correspond with the actual area of common problems.

Sometimes special districts are formed to serve a function which is essential but which state-imposed tax or debt limitations on normal units of local government would make impossible of achievement.

The desire to keep some function "independent of local politics" is often a potent factor. This is particularly true in the case of school districts. Educationists have long maintained that separation from city government is practically a *moral* issue, without thinking too cogently of the disadvantages of divorcing schools from the related complex of other urban services.

The Federal government has sometimes made special districts mandatory. For example, the Soil Conservation Service has insisted that only special districts (in this case, often coterminous with counties) are eligible for its grants. The national public housing agency has specified that only more or less independent local housing authorities can receive federal money. The fact that many other federal agencies have successfully worked through state or local governments would indicate that this concept of the direct federal-special district relationship is not sacrosanct.

However, special districts have, in many instances, been a solution to the problems of "metropolitan areas" noted earlier. St. Louis, that multiple-fractionated unit, has been well served by a Bi-State Development District which has power to construct and operate airports, bridges, tunnels, and terminal facilities, and by a Metropolitan Sewer District. The Port of New York Authority competently handles transportation involving New York and New Jersey. The Metropolitan Sanitary District of Greater Chicago operates in a very large area. (The name is, in itself, interesting. It accepts the fact that peripheral areas are indeed joined "for better or for worse" to the progenitive central city.) The Cleveland Metropolitan Park District includes all of Cuyahoga County and part of an adjacent county. The Metropolitan Water District of Southern California brings water over 350 miles to Los Angeles and its environs from a point in the

Colorado River which is a boundary between California and Arizona.

Obviously, many of these special districts perform important functions. Obviously, many of them are technical subterfuges which in some cases are justified. Nevertheless, they do tend to confuse the concept of local government, and it can be argued that better alternatives could have been found.

Urban Politics

For many decades the politics of large cities has differed markedly from other American politics. It has been less "respectable," probably more corrupt, perhaps less effective in accomplishing its purposes. The unsavory reputation of Tammany Hall, of the Curley regime in Boston, the Vare regime in Philadelphia, and the Nash-Kelley machine in Chicago, lingers in the American memory. Probably for this reason, city government has rarely been a stepping stone to a broader political career. With a few exceptions, such as Rolph of San Francisco, Humphrey of Minneapolis, and Clark of Philadelphia, mayors of large cities have not moved on to governorships or senatorships. Few doubt that Governor Al Smith was handicapped by his connection with New York City politics. Both John F. Kennedy and Robert Kennedy, who had the best possible urban political connections, carefully avoided any semblance of local involvement.

The history of American cities would seem to indicate that the situation results largely from certain ethnic social movements which facilitated the growth of the city machines.

There is no evidence that in Revolutionary times cities were considered particularly badly governed. The original settlers were primarily of Northwestern European stock. The countries from which they came—Great Britain, Holland, Sweden, Germany—were already developing traditions of constitutional government, representative institutions, and even of religious tolerance, and these people quite readily organized democratic machinery for the small cities of their day.

During the nineteenth and first decades of the twentieth centuries, the cities grew enormously in size. The original inhabitants were replaced by Irish, Polish and Russian Jews, Italians, Hungarians, Czechs, Bulgarians, Serbs, Slavs, and others from southeastern Europe. This movement affected the quality of municipal government for many reasons, two of which seem of special importance. First, many of these people valued self-government in a general way, but they had had almost no direct experience with it. The areas from which they came did not emphasize wide popular participation, and the new immigrants did not understand democratic machinery. Second, except for the Irish, these groups generally knew little English. They had practically no money, and they desperately needed help in securing jobs, food, medical care, and housing. Some of this aid was given by a friendly political "machine," which asked only for votes in return. Moreover, the precinct captain was often a sympathetic resource when a member of a family got into some sort of legal trouble. It is small wonder that people in such a situation failed to realize that this benevolent patron was cheating them with corrupt government and failure to meet urgent city problems, and that they continued to be a mainstay of "boss" control.

The power of the boss has declined in recent decades as the immigrant groups have prospered, become better educated, more independent, and have, frequently, moved out into suburbs. However, the tradition of relatively poor government has lasted in many large cities, and there are vestiges of machines or, in a city like Chicago, an entire machine is left. One unfortunate result of the disrepute in which local government is widely held is that even cities which are trying to improve face a built-in distrust. Gans, in his study of Italian Americans in the West End of Boston, portrays an entire group of citizens who feel antagonistic to *all* municipal officials, who believe that "government" is trying to exploit them, in spite of genuine evidence to the contrary.[6]

In many of our central cities, the European ethnic has been replaced in slum areas by the Black American, the Mexican American, and the Puerto Rican. Obviously, residence in a slum is not anyone's "first choice," but in the case of the blacks, it was inescapable for reasons in addition to sheer poverty. Their great movement city-ward occurred during the 1950's as employment opportunities in agriculture decreased. In the urban area, they were kept out of most suburbs by federal regulations, local regulations, and "real estate discrimination." The Federal Housing Agency allowed insurance of mortgages only in areas of similar social and racial background. Local zoning ordinances frequently made it economically impossible for even the steadily employed black to move into the suburbs. The real estate industry often refused to sell or lease to blacks except in areas already, or on the verge of being, predominantly black. The federal rules have now been changed, as have most local regulations, and there are encouraging gaps in private barriers. But past discrimination has, as we shall see, had an effect on the political attitudes of black citizens.

It should be noted that not only does the black face the urban problems with an inadequate education; all too frequently in the past, upward mobility has been blocked by discrimination and therefore education did not seem very worthwhile to him. Moreover, often he did not experience the firm but impartial law enforcement to which most other Americans are accustomed. Both of these factors affect his political outlook. Although there is no indication that black Americans will form "machines" in the old sense, they have not always learned to select first class leaders from their own race, and they are not likely in the immediate future to improve the weak standards of government inherited from the boss era. Any real amelioration for the black city-dweller must come from vastly improved municipal politics. Resentment is understandable, but responsible black leadership must be *constructive*.

Another example of the same sort of problem relates to metropolitan areas. There is some evidence that black majorities in central cities have been opposed to metropolitan developments because they feared that a metropolitan district with an overall white majority would overwhelm the black central city majority. And yet, it is clear that no one suffers more from the lack of

adequately organized metropolitan services than the core-city
occupant. There is already noticeable emigration of more prosperous blacks to the suburbs, and this fact may, in a decade or
so, overcome the racial argument against planning within larger
boundaries.

City Employee Associations

A very important new factor in municipal government is the
organized city employee. The unions quite naturally concern
themselves with salaries, wages, and fringe benefits. (Their demands have probably had much to do with the financial problem
of New York City, discussed in Chapter Six.) But they have also
extended their influence to public policy questions related to
their work. Increasingly, using not only political pressure but
also strikes to attain their ends, they have often become a seriously disruptive force. While, strictly speaking, the dispute between New York City and the organized police group concerned
matters within union jurisdiction, the ensuing strike which left
millions of citizens unprotected for several days is a grim example of the dangers of power without responsibility.

Innumerable other instances could be cited where collective
bargaining rights spill over into areas which should properly not
be union-determined.

In recent months organized teachers in Washington, D.C., under the guise of protesting certain salary incentive provisions,
have aided in scuttling a well-planned effort to improve the education of Washington's predominantly black school children.

In Los Angeles, New York, Boston, San Francisco, Chicago, and
Philadelphia—all cities and counties with strong employee organizations of civil servants—certain intolerable conditions in
public hospitals were reported. While public hospitals certainly
suffer from lack of money, many of the problems of delay and
over-all indifference of hospital personnel (other than doctors)
are related to the entrenched position of union members.[7]

During the single year of 1968, union action significantly determined public policy in New York City in three major instances.[8]

(1) A series of teachers' strikes, called ostensibly because of technical violation of tenure provisions, in effect curtailed the Ocean Hill–Brownsville Demonstration District's experiment in community control of education. (2) "Demonstrations, both in New York City and in Albany, in favor of the liberalization of welfare laws, have occurred with the full participation (if not actual leadership) of the union representing employees of the Department of Social Services." The interesting thing about the recently concluded contract is that the union has agreed, in exchange for a sharp increase in wages, to a substantial reduction in future staffing and to a decrease in eligibility investigations of welfare applicants. Were we not studying idealistic public servants, there might be some suspicion of a "deal." (3) There was a controversy over the establishment of an independent New York City Health and Hospitals Corporation to take over the city's decaying hospital system. The decisive vote was cast by the union of hospital workers. It clearly had a veto power. Its assent was predicated upon two assumptions: a major political decision would always be subject to a union veto; and political bureaucracies and union bureaucracies are engaged in an unending standoff.

Finally, and probably by accident, employee unions have added another complexity to urban problems. Their insistence on higher wages and higher qualifications has often reduced the possibility for the city to employ unskilled ghetto dwellers. Custodial and simple labor jobs become out of reach for those who need them most when there is a quite unnecessary qualification of a high school diploma.

Faulty Attitudes—Faulty Techniques

1. It must be frankly admitted that failure to solve some of the toughest of urban problems is due to unfortunate attitudes on the part of governmental employees. A "friendly" policeman may not be the total solution to crime, but few doubt that the tension between predominantly white police forces and a cohesive black or brown community has exacerbated the difficulty. Many an essentially law-abiding black hesitates to cooperate with a law-enforcement system which he *feels* (rightly or wrongly) to be stacked against his race. It is the author's opinion that much of the current flurry about legitimizing "ghetto English" stems from ineptitude on the part of school teachers. "Ghetto English," like "Cockney English" (see George Bernard Shaw!), or indeed any provincial linguistic variation in European countries, is a respectable method of communication within a limited area. "Standard English" should be presented as a useful way of communication within a somewhat broader area—not as a particularly morally superior way of communication.

Gans, in the study of Italian Boston West Enders already mentioned, discusses an interesting variation of this obtuseness.[9] "The planners and caretakers" (as he calls those engaged in social work in the area) are predominantly upper middle class professionals, and are intellectually incapable of distinguishing between their solid working-class clients and the genuinely under-privileged "lower classes." For this reason, they stress various welfare, recreational, health facilities instead of stressing the development of technical skills for which their clients are already well prepared and which might lead to "craft" status.

2. Many urban problems are bucking a lack of expertise in special fields. For instance—air pollution. Los Angeles County was a pioneer in eliminating "standing" sources of air pollution, and in studying air pollution caused by combustion of moving gasoline engines. Much research is under way—by the auto industry, by universities, and by governmental units. In spite of much emotional rhetoric, most Americans will continue to drive cars; what is needed is a practicable technical break-through which can reconcile ecological theory with everyday convenience.

A second example might be "public housing" as a panacea for everything from crime to unemployment. This was a laudable experiment, and public housing certainly has some value, but experience in Chicago, St. Louis, Newark, and other areas which have substantial public housing projects indicates that crime, unemployment, and sub-standard education remain in an area of well-constructed governmentally-financed residential units.

3. Even though New York and Los Angeles support public school systems well above the national average, they have not solved the problem of raising the general status of their disadvantaged groups. It would seem that our existing expertise is inadequate. Police do not control crime adequately; teachers do not teach adequately; and social workers do not rehabilitate adequately. The author has no taste for "muck-raking." Quite the contrary. Many of the errors are not only honest errors—they are errors based on high idealism. The writer merely wishes to mention that good intentions alone cannot solve certain complicated problems.

The Failures of State Governments to Face Urban Problems

It has already been noted that legal authority over local governments is vested in the state government, which can set limits on local taxing and local borrowing, consolidate or abolish local governments, and determine the operational details of municipal, county, and (in some cases) district units. It would seem, then, that responsibility for the disorganized mess of local government could be dumped peremptorily on the steps of the state capitol. Why should not the state, with its complete legal authority, have legislated model systems of local government, set up rational areas of jurisdiction, concentrated responsibility? The answer is that the state government is itself rather complicated. No one doubts that a strong governor or a strong legislature has great impact, but many state *constitutions* include detailed provisions about county government, even extending to lists of required officials and the method of their election. A few southern states specify that county officials be chosen by the state legislature—a procedure which, in practice, usually means election by the county's delegation.

City governments are usually somewhat freer from controls.

About a third of the states have constitutional "home rule" amendments which permit considerable flexibility as to the form of government, and several other states have general incorporation statutes which eliminate any detailed legislative controls. Nevertheless, even in these cases, municipal financial power is limited, and two other factors further circumscribe the city's independence: (1) as we have already noted, in practice many properly municipal functions must be shared with other local units; (2) courts have further invaded municipal autonomy by frequent decisions that various governmental activities require state-wide action.

The school district, like the county, is a legal creature of the state. It too has freedom of action in some areas, but its entire financial status is subject to state control and potentially the state has power to intervene in any aspect of its operation. Many legislatures have successfully offered financial inducements to consolidation of small districts, but many of the latter still remain too small for efficient operation.

In general, it might be said that the states have done creditable jobs in developing highways and supporting state universities and colleges; medium-level jobs in caring for the mentally ill and prisoners; but very poor jobs in developing rational and efficient local governmental machinery. That is, as we have said before, most flagrantly the case in large urban areas.

There are several reasons which might explain the mediocre performance of the state legislatures, and before criticizing them too sharply, we must bear in mind that, in addition to setting low salaries, most constitutions limit the *length of legislative sessions* so that detailed and thoughtful consideration of complex problems is made more difficult. It may be, as Paul Ylvisacker has suggested, that highways and state universities were things which a non-urban legislator could understand, while the intricate problems of slums and welfare were beyond his scope.[10] It must also be realized that it is impossible to set any rigid pattern for *the* best form of local government. Conditions vary widely among cities and counties, and few general experts are rash enough to pronounce definitely precisely which kind of arrangement would work best in each particular case. Each is in need of specific study. It is ungenerous to expect the great mass of state legislators to have both the pertinent knowledge and the wisdom necessary to avoid mistakes.

The writer is inclined to think that the basic problem has been the inability of both legislators and governors to understand the changes being undergone within the state, particularly in large metropolitan areas. The debacle of our cities has come quite rapidly—a matter of a few decades. Cities have not had adequate representation to present their problems, and in many cases, the cities themselves have not developed constructive programs which they successfully defend. These are obstacles which must be overcome, because it still remains true that the states have the ultimate authority. They certainly have the responsibility. They must either assume active leadership or encourage strong local leadership with which they can thoughtfully cooperate.

Financial Impasse

Perhaps not all urban problems could be solved by money, but a good many could be ameliorated, and the stark fact is that cities lack adequate resources to perform even their basic functions well. Crime could be more nearly controlled if police forces were greatly augmented and much inner-city opposition to law enforcement could be reduced if policemen were better trained for the necessarily difficult role they play. But more policemen and better educated policemen cost more money than is available to the average large city.

The same is true in other fields. The real solution to the welfare problem probably lies in a combination of expensive job-training and expensive inducements for getting back to work. Our big city schools, dealing so largely with the disadvantaged, should spend twice as much money per child as the wealthy suburbs. Instead, they spend far less.[11] Housing improvement can be achieved only by enormously expensive projects. A third to a half of non-white housing in our bigger cities has been classified as deteriorating or dilapidated, but none of our major cities could afford to repair or replace these quarters.[12]

A basic difficulty is that the city is not in a privileged position as a fund raiser. Both the central government and the state governments can collect taxes more easily because they cover a broader area. Few of us would emigrate from the United States merely to save on taxes. Few Californians would leave their sun-drenched state because North Dakota's tax levies were smaller. But almost anyone would move across a municipal border into surrounding territory where the tax burden was substantially less. As a result, the only resources of the city are the individuals or businesses who feel forced to remain. General property taxes can be, and often are, extremely high, but they constitute practically the only base.

The obvious result of this situation is a continuing downward spiral. As the city's lack of funds causes poorer schools, poorer law enforcement, poorer general maintenance, more middle class people leave, and the tax base shrinks further. There have been actual municipal bankruptcies; there will be more. Then all the problems multiply, and the left-over inhabitants face not expanding, but actually contracting, opportunities for advancement.

Economics of the City

Many books have been written around the thesis that underlying *all* urban problems are the basic facts of economics. It is impossible here to do more than summarize this viewpoint, which, on the whole, tends to feel that sociological approaches neglect too cavalierly urban economics.

1. Every city has its own purely economic problems. In the seventeenth and eighteenth centuries, Charleston, South Carolina, was one of the largest port cities in Colonial America, until its exports of rice, indigo, and tobacco became commercially less important. New Orleans was a rival of New York in the first part of the nineteenth century until the Erie Canal directed mid-western agricultural produce through the port of New York rather than down-river to New Orleans. Boston was declining as an industrial center in the early 1940's, but technical developments introduced in its *out-lying* areas, partially revived the city as a focus of business and industry. It is clear that if business and commerce decline, the entire economy of a city is affected. Unemployment, declining land values, and lower tax base—all are related.

2. As we have seen, an entire city may be affected by economic factors. But within a city, certain areas may also be affected. This is not a simple problem. An older area may become obsolescent because newer, expensive areas tend to supplant it; but it may be that some few families fail to maintain their homes and gardens, and the entire neighborhood thereby declines. New suburbs do attract the wealthier citizens who desire more space; but high taxes in the central city, and poor urban planning, may discourage many who would prefer urban living. It is probable that very few urban housing areas will have their present social and economic status a quarter-century from now. And, of course, as a section goes "down-hill," it becomes less and less of a tax-resource for the city, and, in the later stages, its cost to the city for education, health, welfare, and crime control increases.

On the other hand, occasionally a reverse process takes place. In parts of New York's East Side and in Washington's Georgetown, what was once a decaying community is now very elite. The factors in these cases are complicated. Certainly, "economic pressures" suggested more valuable use of this favorably placed land, but the same logic has not been effective in other potential slums. Less sociologically involved are the cases where Federal Urban Renewal Projects—discussed elsewhere—have rejuvenated certain urban areas.

3. Individuals, like cities and neighborhoods, react to economic factors, and it is not always easy to understand the differing reactions. It is certainly true that some who live in unhealthy, crime-ridden slums, who seem not to gain much value from their public schooling, become increasingly worse off. It is also true, as we have noted several times, that some ghetto-dwellers in the past have shown remarkable upward mobility. Clearly, economics is not the sole determinant, but it is an important one. Moreover, it should be remembered that even those groups who speedily moved out of the slums had, *while they were there,* a higher crime rate than before or after. Thus, large expenditures for various governmental functions will always be necessary in the inner-city.

FUNCTIONS AND LEVELS OF GOVERNMENT

The United States Constitution specifically lists exclusively federal functions such as the power to wage war, to raise and equip armies, to control interstate commerce, to negotiate with foreign nations, etc. According to the Tenth Amendment: "The powers not delegated to the United States by the Constitution, nor prohibited by it to the States, are reserved to the States respectively, or to the people." For the large part of American history, this allocation was followed—with, of course, many functions turned over by the states to their legal "creatures," the local units. The Supreme Court enforced the arrangement rather strictly and fairly vigorously until the last half century, although it did allow the interstate commerce clause to be expanded to include a wide variety of business and labor regulations. (Of course, the 1964 Civil Rights decision affected many aspects of state and local government, but this came after the trend toward centralization was well under way.)

The development of the grants-in-aid system, however, practically eliminated any sharp demarcation between the powers reserved to certain levels of government. Congress may, through its financial sponsorship, enter any field of governmental operation which it deems desirable. It is true that the states are still constitutionally barred from enumerated federal powers, but this is no very critical issue since they have neither the financial resources nor any particular incentive to encroach on most federal functions.

This chapter will discuss a few of the major governmental functions which have impact on the urban problem, to point out where responsibility lies, and in some cases to suggest realignments. However, it should be stressed that no rigid allocation is workable or desirable. An important change in the technology of disease control, for instance, could suddenly create a predominantly federal concern in what had formerly been a municipal public health problem. A marked change in public opinion could well shift decision-making on urban renewal from federal to local officials. There should always remain a large element of fluidity.

On the other hand, far too many political scientists have ignored the problem of allocation of functions to various levels of government. During the 1930's, there was a mass of literature on federal-municipal relations. The writers were so enchanted with the possibilities of direct federal-local projects that they entirely overlooked the fact that the states are *legally* responsible for the lower levels of government. Thus the very great statutory and moderate financial powers of the states to assist in many of these programs was sacrificed. It is very probable that the slow and unsatisfactory progress of public housing and urban renewal is in part a result of failure to recognize how great a potential interest the states have in this field.

Another group of writings which has neglected, even rejected, the allocation of functions follows the so-called "marble-cake theory" of the late Morton Grodzins. This theory maintained that functions could not be neatly disposed like the layers of a layer cake, but must be dispersed among various levels of government in the irregular, sometimes unpredictable, pattern found in marble cakes. This viewpoint is largely correct in what it maintained—the problem lies in what it leaves unsaid. If a function was not to be allocated to one level of government, which level should be responsible for it? In the web of bureaucratic inter-level relationships inherent in marble-cake government, where was the will of the people to find any expression or any control? Moreover, popular support of, popular participation in, government programs is of immeasurable importance to their success; but government by inter-level administrative agreements leaves no scope for a feeling of popular participation or even popular interest.

This is not to say that responsibility is an uncomplicated unitary thing. In the following pages, it will be evident that there are differing kinds of primary responsibility. It is perfectly possible that the primary *legal* responsibility for a given function may rest with one level of government, the primary *financial* responsibility with another level, and the primary *administrative* responsibility with a third. This situation might seem as confusing to the public as the marble-cake theory. However, an attempt will be made to distinguish carefully among the various types of responsibility and, in some cases, to indicate what level probably should have the predominant control if the urban problem is to be solved.

Public Welfare

Although there are many private and semi-public philanthropic agencies, America, like other civilized countries, recognizes that government does have some obligation to care for the poor and the unfortunate. For many decades, public welfare was considered a strictly local responsibility with no federal and only limited state support. During the 1930's, the New Deal recognized a federal responsibility, but it seems never to have been very clear as to how much of the federal role was strictly financial and how much was policy-determining. Since the mid-thirties, the national government has made grants for various "categories"—old age assistance, aid to the blind, aid to dependent children. Usually the states add some money (about a third of the total cost), and the cities and counties pay the rest. The local units handle the actual administration under federal and/or state supervision. Insurance for the aged (in contrast to welfare payments) is administered directly by the federal government. Direct general relief, apart from the "categories," has been a state and local responsibility.

It is obvious that such an arrangement confuses the accountability of the various levels of government. Nevertheless, some participation of federal, state, and local levels is essential. Welfare requires substantial central financing in a country like ours where economic prosperity fluctuates rapidly, where areas may vary widely in their ability to shoulder the necessary costs, and where people can readily move to the jurisdiction which pays the

highest benefits. (The latter practice, by the way, has been encouraged by Supreme Court decisions). On the other hand, welfare requires some local direction if it is to be effectively coordinated with education, employment offices, public health,
housing, and policing.

As this book is being written, the Congress is considering the
alternative welfare scheme described elsewhere which will assist some cities financially, but may further delay the effective
inter-relationship of welfare policy with that of other governmental agencies. Some of the proposed legislation provides for
direct federal administration in certain cases. This bodes ill for
coordination, since a federal bureau is far more likely to follow
the policy of the Congressional Committees which control its
operations and its financing than it is to work seriously toward
integrating its policy with that of other bureaus.

It is to be hoped that, in the future, the national government,
while assuming much of the financial responsibility in such a
field as welfare, will be wise enough to keep any controls flexible
enough to encourage rather than prevent local experimentation.
The cities obviously have a deep interest both in efficient administration and in thoughtful integration of welfare with the
other related services mentioned above. In many cases, the
county and not the city administers welfare, but even then the
city is involved. It must mesh many of its purely municipal functions with the county welfare program. Moreover, where welfare
costs are met in part by county property taxes, there is an obvious
impact on the tax resources of the city.

Public Health

Perhaps because public health is a less controversial subject
than other functions, perhaps because it is a field which clearly
does not recognize arbitrary boundary lines (an epidemic is not
a *local* issue!), most aspects of the public health service have
been rather well coordinated among the various levels of government. In the 1930's, when the present inter-level method of administrative operation was initiated, the national Public Health

Service sensibly decided to work through the states and counties. Grants were used to establish close working relationships. Personnel move fairly freely between state and national levels. While the bulk of administration is handled by local units, there is close cooperation with state and national health agencies, which assume legal and financial responsibilities. Although certain specific aspects may require greater expenditures in some areas, the general framework as it now exists is probably adequate to handle urban problems in disease prevention and control.

Unfortunately, the record of hospitalization is less satisfactory. Most urban areas maintain one or two public hospitals for the use of the poor, but these are often inconveniently located in old and inadequate buildings and are frequently staffed with undertrained and bureaucratically indifferent personnel. The federal government has long made grants for hospital construction, and currently, of course, Medicare pays much of the cost of hospital operation, but neither of the upper levels has shown any consistent efforts to improve hospital administration.

Public Safety

Traditionally in America, law enforcement has been highly decentralized. There are a few specialized federal police forces, and one of them, the Federal Bureau of Investigation, has for several decades gathered statistics for, and provided some training programs for, state and local law enforcement officers. A new agency in the Department of Justice, the Office of Law Enforcement Assistance, has since 1965 administered a few small grants to states and localities. The Armed Forces of the United States are rarely used directly to back up local agencies, but they do equip, train, and partially pay the National Guard which has been less infrequently called out by the states to assist in local crises.

More than a dozen of the states have state police forces which cooperate fairly closely with local law enforcement agencies; but the unions, fearing that state police might be employed in strike-breaking, have effectively stopped any extension of these units. Most states do, however, have special highway patrols.

Thus, by far the bulk of law enforcement responsibility is carried by city or county officers who vary widely in quality and training. Through radio, teletype, and other mechanical means, adjacent jurisdictions cooperate quite closely in the pursuit of criminals.

It is no exaggeration, however, to say that law enforcement is one of the weakest phases of American government. Crime rates appear to be much higher than in other countries of similar educational and industrial development; an alarming percentage of criminals is never apprehended; and a very small percentage is actually convicted. "Organized crime" has become an important factor in some areas. As noted in Chapter Two, the over-all quality of life, especially in the central cities, is seriously affected by the prevalence of crime. In an atmosphere of constant physical fear, it is difficult to develop in the citizens the interest in education, in economic advancement, and in community cohesion which is essential to permanent solution to urban problems.

Why has our country done so poorly in this field? Several factors may be relevant. We are working with large masses of people who are probably more widely divergent in ethnic, educational, and economic background than is the case in large cities in other parts of the world. A tradition of "frontier violence" combined with an insistence on the practically unrestricted right to possess fire-arms may be another element. But there is little doubt in the writer's mind that our overly decentralized law enforcement system is a major contributor to the unfortunate situation. It would seem that in this case we have put too much stress on this valuable concept of local control, just as in other cases we have put too little. Substantial federal grants are needed to upgrade pay, education, and training of local officers. States need to develop or expand their own police forces—which would work closely in support of the local ones. Judicial and correctional machinery, almost entirely outside the province of local jurisdictions, should be vastly improved if there is to be any reasonable relation between apprehension and judgment and punishment of the suspect.

Public Education

We tend to equate public education with local school districts. It is true that these do handle most of the administration and sometimes carry most of the financial cost. But it must be remembered that for many decades the *primary* legal responsibility has rested with the state governments, which contain in their constitutions no "home rule restrictions" which apply to school districts.

Many local school districts, especially those in central city areas with which this book is chiefly concerned, do not have the financial resources to support what their citizens consider adequate schools or to pay what their teachers believe to be adequate salaries. Accordingly, all states have developed some form of financial aid. The range is wide. Two states contribute almost 100% of the costs; others less than 25%. Usually some degree of extra support is supplied for the poorer areas, but the "equalization" is not often truly equitable. Wealthy suburbs, utilizing mostly their own resources, can maintain much more effective schools than can the central city, even with greater state aid. The process becomes dismally circular. The urban core must spend far more per capita for welfare, law enforcement, public health, and similar functions. It therefore has far less to allocate for education—in just the areas where effective schools are most needed.

Costs of higher education are sometimes divided between municipal governments and the states, chiefly in the case of municipal universities or junior colleges. However, much the greatest part of public higher education is supported by the state alone.

The federal government contributes altogether a few billion dollars, but its role in public education is analogous to the process by which a man slowly enters a cold swimming pool. He constantly gets in a little deeper, occasionally retreating or perhaps lifting one arm completely out—temporarily. It is hard to find any pattern. Some support has been given to state land-grant universities for over a century. Grants for buildings, for student aid, for research, and for other *specific* things have been allocated to both independent and public institutions of higher education. Federal funds have helped elementary and secondary schools with buildings, school lunch programs, aid to disadvantaged areas, and many educational studies.

Certainly, at the moment, the problem of the urban schools is not being satisfactorily met. The Advisory Commission on Intergovernmental Relations has suggested that the states assume all financial responsibilities, thus freeing local tax income for the many other pressing needs. This approach seems sound to the writer, although some federal aid should undoubtedly be extended to the poorer states. Unfortunately, the states do not seem likely to adopt this recommendation in the near future, but until some such re-organization is instituted the schools in the central cities will, on the whole, continue sub-standard.

Streets and Highways

Responsibility in this important field has been shared by the three levels of government for over a half-century. Federal grants have been made to the states for the construction of major interstate routes—many of which, of course, are of local importance. Until recently, the grants were based on 50% of the cost, but in the new interstate system, they have risen to 90%. States have their own gas tax and auto license revenues, earmarked for road construction. Thus they are able to meet the requirements of the federal grants and also to build their own routes when this seems desirable. Most states share some of their revenues with counties and cities. However, since local units have no taxes which are specifically tied to road and street construction and maintenance, the allocations in the general budget for these purposes are usually inadequate. It is a common experience, after having driven hundreds of miles on bumpless well-graded inter-state highways, to be literally jolted by the condition of streets in what seems to be a prosperous city.

There have been important urban side effects of recent federal and state highway programs through or around cities. For one thing, they have removed substantial areas from other uses and from the city tax rolls. Moreover, they have encouraged the settlement of city workers in dormitory suburbs. This movement in turn has had two results. Wealthier citizens tend to move farther and farther away; their tax resources are lost to the central city; and their interest in urban problems declines. The mass entrance and exit of workers twice a day increases the problems of air pollution and traffic control. Belatedly the federal government is at least trying to help with the latter difficulty by giving financial aid to metropolitan rapid transit.

On the whole, the present allocation of financing and administrative responsibilities has not proved too bad, and it is likely to continue. It is to be hoped, however, that both federal and state highway planners will in the future give more thoughtful attention to the enormous social and economic consequences of programs which were often viewed by the planners merely in engineering terms.

Private and Public Housing, Urban Renewal

In probably no other area of governmental functions is the allocation of responsibility as chaotic and as unsatisfactory as in that of housing in general.

Almost all cities and some counties have ordinances governing the construction and maintenance of housing. The construction regulations are usually rigidly enforced because many unions and many contractors have an interest in their enforcement. Rules for maintenance of building quality and those providing against over-crowding are frequently ignored. In all fairness, it should be noted that this laxity is not always a result of cynical indifference. Sometimes municipal authorities hesitate to demand expensive repairs which would necessarily raise rents and perhaps deprive the really poor of even that good a home.

The federal government has given a gigantic boost to the private building of residences, especially in the suburbs, through guaranteeing mortgages on home construction. This federal insurance (frequently called F.H.A. because it has been administered through the Federal Housing Administration) has, however, had no substantial impact on the core cities, because of various restrictions concerning the type of area in which the insured house is to be built.

A few states, notably New York, have displayed some initiative in state public housing projects. Practically no city has had the cash or credit to enter the public housing field on its own. The federal government has, since the mid 1930's, made grants to local authorities for some public housing but it started out with a most unfortunate policy. The original Public Housing Administration was deeply mistrustful of state and local politics, and established local "housing authorities" which were as independent as possible of the local authorities and totally independent of the state governments. As noted elsewhere, this arrangement, the exact opposite of that followed by public health and highway grant agencies, has been a serious handicap in the development of public housing in the United States.

The urban renewal program, developed since 1949, somewhat altered this pattern. Urban renewal projects had to secure local consent. Cities which would gain much from the increased property values were willing and eager to cooperate in all aspects. Thus there was much more truly local administration involved than in public housing.

Fiscal responsibility for public housing must obviously rest with the federal government, or with some of the wealthier states, because of their stronger financial position or credit status. But administrative responsibility for construction should be vested in the cities which have control over the closely related field of city planning and with the states which are slowly developing a sense of the importance of metropolitan planning.

Summary

The division of the three major types of responsibility among the three major levels of government does undoubtedly complicate the urban problem. For instance, functions like highways, housing, and welfare over which the cities most need control are largely out of their hands because the financial responsibility rests with state and/or national governments. There is one encouraging trend recently, however—a trend away from the ever-increasing centralization advocated in the thirties and fifties. More and more Congressmen are coming to the purely practical conclusion that the federal government simply cannot run everything. It will, of course, as it must, continue to intervene in state and local affairs through grants, but it is not likely to take over active administration of many new functions. And it is likely that Congress will, either through some form of block grants or some form of revenue sharing, take the most sensible approach: turn over to the cities money to spend in ways best suited to meet the particular needs of each area.

FEDERAL HELP—
SCATTERED SHOTS

4 ★
★
★

When considering the critical need for vastly increased urban expenditures, it is quite natural to think first of the Federal government as a source of financial help. After all, the national budget appropriates over $200 billion, while total state and local budgets amount to only $125 billion. Moreover, the Federal government relies chiefly on income taxes, which are elastic, that is, they rise with the economy; and, on the other hand, when revenues are falling, its control of the banking system and of other aspects of the economy enable it to borrow more easily than can states or localities. Finally, the fact that Congress covers the broadest possible area and is farthest removed from individual taxpayers, makes its appropriations less susceptible to narrower political reprisals.

Federal Expenditures in Urban Areas

In fact, the Federal government is currently spending the rather substantial amount of about $27 billion a year on various urban projects.[1] As we shall discuss more fully a little later, these funds are divided among several hundred specific "grants-in-aid," but here we shall merely summarize a few of the general categories.

1. Almost a third of a billion dollars is spent on the donation of agricultural commodities.

2. Commerce and transportation assistance totals over three billion, of which over two and a half billion goes to highways. It might be noted that the freeways which encircle or cross your nearest big city were financed by the Federal government often at a very high cost per mile.

3. Various community and housing projects account for two and three-quarter billion dollars. About two billion of this amount goes for urban renewal—which may, somewhat simplistically, be defined as the destruction of old buildings to permit construction of more modern and more expensive ones. Public housing, which receives over a half billion, is concerned chiefly with new construction, but does include some continuing subsidies. Model Cities programs, which receive about a quarter billion dollars, are relatively new and somewhat more complex. They are being tried in 150 cities and are an attempt to affect the quality of life in depressed areas through improvement of job, housing, educational, and health opportunities.

4. Elementary and secondary education receive a billion and a half dollars—chiefly intended to assist school districts which face problems of poorer children.

5. About a third of a billion is allocated to the administration of unemployment compensation and employment offices; and various "manpower activities"—vocational training and related programs—receive over a billion.

6. More than three billion dollars is used for various health subsidies, of which over two thirds is for medical assistance.

7. Income security accounts for five and a half billion dollars, of which practically all goes for public assistance. This basic outlay keeps increasing despite hopes that it would be reduced by other programs.

8. Finally, there is a quarter billion subsidy for "general government," about half of which is designated for a new program attempting to help cities with crime control and law enforcement.

Whereas, obviously, no city would wish to lose these grants without gaining some comparable financial assistance, both officials and most students of municipal government feel that the existing system has woefully failed in what is, after all, its main purpose: the over-all improvement of urban conditions. Only a little over two billion is paid directly to city governments. Before attention is turned to recent or projected alternative approaches, some comments on the "grants-in-aid" mechanism seem appropriate.

Grants-in-Aid Mechanism

The natural superiority of the Federal government as a tax-raising agency has already been noted. But the state and local governments have the constitutional authority for, and are the practicable political and administrative levels for, the administration of such functions as education, health, recreation, welfare, housing standards, law enforcement, etc. The question is not *whether* the most efficient fund-raising level of government should disburse money to the levels responsible for fund-needing activities. In other federal countries like Canada and Australia, there are extensive federal grants to states, federal grants to localities, state grants to local units. The question is *how* this disbursal should function.

The distinctive feature of the American system is excessive fragmentation of grants, and this may be related to the American concept of separation of powers.

In Parliamentary federal countries, the "Chief Executive" of the central government is the head of the controlling legislative majority, and in turn, the "executive" of each subsidiary unit represents his own established majority. For this reason, a solution arrived at by political "executives" is per se a legislative *fait accompli*. But in the United States, neither could the President "deliver" the Congress nor could the Governor "deliver" his legislature. There are undoubted advantages to this legislative independence, but it is obvious that it leaves in Congress an excellent opportunity to pursue a multitude of pet good causes. Individual legislators (or groups) can secure a quarter billion here, a half billion there, for some projects in which they are especially interested. Typically the programs are worked out between the Congressmen concerned and a few administrators in the appropriate bureau or department, and both work in close conjunction with the pressure groups in the field. Typically also, the dedicated legislator, encouraged by "experts," tries to include conditions which will keep the grant "out of local politics." The goal may be laudable, but it is apparent that the result is a series of unrelated subsidies which are in no way integrated into any over-all municipal plan and which remain financially and, to some extent, administratively independent of state or local officials.[2]

It is probably true that most writers, preoccupied with their specific fields, would support the specialized grant. Certainly Bailey and Mosher are eloquent in its defense, and quite frankly cite as one advantage its value in removing power from the local governments and concentrating it in the Congressmen-pressure group nexus.[3]

The people who are administering the cities and the school districts are much less enthusiastic. They find themselves responsible for literally several hundred specific grants. Reports, accounting, and program planning must be adjusted to the varying requirements of the federal (and sometimes state) agencies which are in actual control of the funds. Added to the burden of this redundant administrative work is the sad fact that frequently the terms of the grants do not meet the needs of a particular area. After all, it is hardly reasonable to expect that a formula devised in Washington is equally applicable in Chicago, Illinois and Jackson, Mississippi.

Even more ironic is the fact that many federal grants are working at cross purposes with other federal grants. For example, the federal insurance of mortgages (FHA) made possible a tremendous expansion of housing, almost entirely in the suburbs. This accelerated, if it did not initiate, the flow of population outward from the central city. The federally financed inter-state highway program made it easier to commute—if one had a car. But the new highway systems competed with public transport systems. The result is evident. Public transport systems are dying—where they are not already dead. The central city resident who is too poor to own a car (or, in the case of working couples, *two* cars) is stranded. When one adds that industry is moving out from the central city, the problem of transportation is intensified. So now the federal government is beginning to make grants for mass transportation.

Highway programs are apparently also in conflict with Model

City programs. A recent study indicates that federal highways have been routed through inner city areas which had been set off as federal experiments in urban rejuvenation.[4]

Recent Changes in Grant Mechanisms

The Safe Streets Act of 1968 is one example of a new willingness on the part of the Federal government to trust the judgment of state and local officials. The original Act authorized $63 million to be spent on crime control, and subsequent appropriations have been substantially increased. These funds were to cover action grants, planning grants, academic assistance, research and development, and FBI programs. The significant aspect of this program is that it both required the states to establish *state* law enforcement planning agencies, and authorized block grants to *states,* leaving them authority to distribute the funds among localities or regions. There have been many criticisms of the administration of these grants by some states and this particular attempt to involve states in the urban problems may not be the perfect solution.[5] However, the Advisory Commission on Intergovernmental Relations has recommended continuance of this approach.[6]

It seems obvious that federal aid should be greatest where the need is greatest and the local tax resources lowest. While there should be care to avoid subsidizing uneconomic units, some equalization is desirable. After all, citizens from Arkansas and Mississippi (two low per-capita income states) go out to other parts of the country, and it is to the general interest as well as to theirs that they should be able to furnish adequate educational and health services to their young people. Long indifferent to this factor of equalization, grants legislation is beginning to face the problem, and, as the Office of Management and Budget points out, is allocating more per capita to states with low per capita income. Unfortunately, the development of suitable formulae for distribution is extremely complex, and the frequent result is to freeze the allocation of federal monies into patterns. For instance, urban areas which happen to lie within high per capita income states may receive less help than their very urgent problems would justify.

Block Grants and Revenue Sharing

The Nixon Administration has proposed a measure which would permit consolidation of grants into functional block grants. It would probably be possible to cut the existing four or five hundred grants to twenty or thirty general categories if the project were vigorously pushed and if Congress did not veto it through a resolution. (We have mentioned before, and shall discuss again later the fact that some Congressmen seem to feel a vested interest in specific grants.)

The strongest argument in favor of block grants is the relief from the confusing maze of the present system. Federal funds could be secured more simply by state and local governments; reporting costs would be lessened by reduction of the innumerable and frequently quite dissimilar procedures now required for various grants; preparation of state and local budgets would be vastly simplified. Block grants would, however, leave the national government more control than would the revenue-sharing plan discussed below. Under them, the national government could still exert financial pressure to force states to spend more on welfare, on health, on public works, or on education. Some scholars in the field and some officials believe that this might be advantageous. The federal government would have the power to implement a national policy for expansion of one or more of these functions, while bureau chiefs in Washington would no longer be able to dictate to states or localities the detailed percentages which must be allocated to each small aspect of an over-all program.

Revenue sharing involves the return to the states and localities of either a percentage of the federal tax income, or of fixed sums. It can include, as does the proposal supported by the present administration, a "pass through" of a substantial amount of the shared revenue to local units of a certain size, including, of course, those urban areas with which this booklet is concerned.

Interestingly, its proponents have included a wide spectrum of political viewpoints: Senator Barry Goldwater during the 1964 Presidential campaign; Professor Walter Heller, Chairman of the Council of Economic Advisors during the Johnson regime; the Advisory Commission on Intergovernmental Relations; and now the Nixon Administration.

The figure of $5 billion, beginning in fiscal 1972, and to be increased later, has been suggested as an initial sum by the Administration—an approach also supported by the Advisory Committee on Intergovernmental Relations. Governor Rockefeller of New York vigorously advocates an initial allocation of $10 billion. Certainly if the Rockefeller proposal should be adopted, a real impact on the urban problem is possible. On the assumption that about one third of the total would be passed through to the major cities, the latter would receive over $3 billion—more than all existing grants for community housing and urban development. How significant this could be is evident when we realize that it would constitute about 10% of local budgets.

At the time when this is being written, it is not at all certain that revenue sharing will be approved by Congress. Representative Wilbur Mills, Chairman of the powerful Ways and Means Committee of the House of Representatives, is strongly opposed. Scholars, columnists, reporters, legislators—all are writing copiously for or against the proposal. Perhaps the major argument in its favor is the opportunity for state and local governments to spend federal money on their own most pressing needs—which vary from area to area—without being hamstrung by the detailed provisions of specialized grants. Perhaps the major argument against revenue sharing—a point used by Representative Mills and Professor Lowell Harriss of Columbia University—is that it divorces the responsibility for fund raising from the responsibility for fund disbursal. Theoretically, this is a very cogent criticism. However, it overlooks the practical problem that in many cases local finances are in a truly desperate situation. There *are* certain states and certain cities which have not tapped all possible sources of revenue, but there are also many which have little recourse except to federal funds. There is one argument frequently used to which this writer wishes to enter a strong dissent. It is that state and local governments cannot be "trusted" to carry out the intent of Congress in use of the shared revenue. Many years of service with the federal government, various state governments, and local units would indicate that none of the administrative agencies encountered has a monopoly on conscientious fulfillment of its prescribed duties. It has, on the other hand, been charged that Congressmen are loathe to relinquish the "political" advantages gained by supporting specific grants popular among their particular constituencies. This may be true in certain instances, but the writer is confident that this is a minor factor.

What seems evident is that *some* form of revenue sharing or of intelligently devised block grants is ultimately inevitable in the United States. Every other federal system in the world utilizes them. The current problem is whether this solution will be adopted too late to help in the present urban crisis.

Proposed Federal Welfare Legislation

Also not yet enacted are certain proposals which would rationalize the current chaos of federal, state, and local welfare programs.

The existing "categorical" grants to the aged, the blind, and the disabled would be combined and administered as one unit within the welfare system. A minimum of $110 per month would be guaranteed. Federal payments would be increased, but in some cases larger state and local contributions would be necessary to meet the base figure.

The most important aspect of the new legislation, however, is the "family assistance plan." This is intended to provide basic payments to low-income families with children according to provisions which would encourage employment, would promote family stability, and would tend to equalize nation-wide standards of support. All needy families would receive $500 annually for each two members and $300 each for additional members. This is certainly less than what some states are currently paying to families with dependent children, but it is more than what some poorer states (especially in the South) are spending. Earnings up to $720 a year would be disregarded entirely; earnings above that figure would result in graduated reductions in aid.

There is one clear advantage: namely, in promoting family stability. It is almost universally acknowledged that many quite decent men "desert" their families, because this makes it easier for the mother to secure aid.

There are many unsolved questions, however. Does the $720 figure of maximum earned income to be completely disregarded offer sufficient inducement to get off the welfare rolls? Would national welfare standards, which would certainly reduce the incentive to come to northern and western cities where assistance payments are currently much higher, also reduce the standards for those legitimately domiciled in high cost areas?

Model Cities and Community Action Programs

Even within the federal government, there has been a growing suspicion that the elaborate network of specialized grants has failed to solve the urban problems, and during the last decade, two programs have been initiated which were designed to pull together some of the grants into more integrated community projects and to increase citizen participation in community action. The Model Cities Program of the Department of Housing and Urban Development and the Community Action programs sponsored by the Office of Economic Opportunity will here be very briefly discussed.

Model City grants are made to about 150 municipalities, with appropriations of over four hundred million dollars authorized for fiscal 1972. Cities were supposed to have considerable freedom in the use of the money, subject only to HUD approval. Thus vocational education might be strengthened in a particular school system, a recreation building might be constructed, new approaches to welfare might be tried out. In practice, the elaborate "guidelines" laid down by the Department have seriously restricted any true flexibility in meeting local needs. Even after a recent revision and "reduction," the regulations fill forty single-spaced pages![7]

Community Action programs—devised for the laudable purpose of involving local citizens in the actual processes of self-government—were to receive a half billion dollars in fiscal 1971; less in 1972. So far as the actual functions involved and supported, these often overlap the Model Cities programs. Professor Daniel P. Moynihan has written a thoughtful but discouraging evaluation in his *Maximum Feasible Misunderstanding*. It would appear that the basic difficulty involves political clashes between the representatives of citizen groups and the local officials. This question of citizen participation is, however, of vital importance, and we shall return to it in a later chapter. If the existing arrangement is not successful, other methods must be tried.

Urban Renewal

Since 1949, the federal government has been experimenting with ways to assist the cities with one of their most pressing economic and sociological problems—the decaying central area. The usual procedure is approximately as follows: the city's housing authority, or a special redevelopment authority, buys all the land in a depressed area. The Federal government meets most of the cost. Buildings are razed and the land is sold—at perhaps a quarter of the cost—to a developer who agrees to build apartment houses or office buildings in accordance with a city plan. Ideally, everyone benefits. The developer makes a profit. The city exchanges low tax-income property for high tax-income modern commercial or residential units. The general citizen gains a more attractive central city. The process of deterioration has been arrested, and in some cases a reverse trend begins. The section may become not only economically but socially upgraded.

If all went well, the federal subsidy would be extremely productive. However, all has not always gone well. Many difficulties have been encountered, of which two are of prime importance.

The process has been much slower than was anticipated. If a developer could not be found, or a developer withdrew, the city was left with what the older generation refers to as "Hiroshima flats"—expanses of blocks on which all buildings have been destroyed and no new construction started.

The second problem is far more complex. Many slum inhabitants did not want to leave—for a variety of reasons. It was frequently impossible for them to find any other dwellings at the low rents to which they had become accustomed and which were as much as they could afford. When housing could be located, it might be in an area where transportation to possible work was inaccessible. Sometimes, there was a disinclination to "spread out"—to leave the friends and relatives who had been their neighbors. Moreover, small businesses which were dependent on ethnic ties could not easily relocate, and many owners lost even their marginal economic independence. The federal government has increasingly recognized that this problem of "displaced persons" is serious, and successive statutes have both offered more liberal benefits for relocation and insisted that urban renewal grants should not be issued until practicable arrangements have been made for transfer of slum inhabitants.

In summary, urban renewal has achieved some positive results and should certainly not be written off. But equally certainly, it is a slow and devious, not a fast and simple, cure for the problems of the inner city.

Federal-Local Relations

During the 1930's, when the Federal government was making its first grants directly to cities, the bulk of the published books and articles expressed approbation. Constantly recurring was the thesis that the malapportioned state legislatures neither understood nor were concerned about urban problems. Ergo, the perfect solution was direct federal-city relations, by-passing the states.

In retrospect, much of this literature seems naive. The experience of forty years would seem to indicate that Washington is no more omniscient than Albany, Springfield, or Sacramento. Moreover, the basic legal fact remains that the states have legal power over their subsidiary units. The need was not to divorce, but to marry, federal financial aid and state legal authority. Some of the western Leagues of Cities are turning more toward this tripartite partnership idea. California, the largest and most effective, has recently decided that federal funds for cities could not only be *safely* but most *effectively* channelled through the state government.

Analysis

As we have seen in the course of this chapter, there tend to be three major viewpoints in regard to the role of federal funds in the solution of urban problems.

The first is advocated by most social reform pressure groups, many bureaucrats with specialized interests, and most "liberal" Congressmen. They simply insist that the $27 billion a year currently being spent by the Federal government on urban areas for highways, community development, housing, education, health, and welfare is not enough. This represents only a little over 10% of our national budget, they argue, and should be augmented. Increase the *number* of special grants, increase the *amount* of the various special grants, and urban problems will eventually disappear.

City officials and students of public administration in general take a different view. They maintain that, under the present system, federal grants are too numerous, too subdivided, too uncoordinated, and too erratic to be of much help to any given city in solving its particular difficulties. They advocate either rationally organized block grants or shared revenues which permit a maximum of flexibility for local planning. The Nixon administration has endorsed this approach and has presented an elaborate scheme of revenue sharing with states and larger cities, but it is at present uncertain whether sufficient Congressional support can be mustered.

Another viewpoint, advanced by a divergent group of people,

is that urban problems must ultimately be settled by economic factors which are not necessarily related to governmental policies. It might in general be said that this reaction is shared by "conservatives" in both political parties. They are not particularly in favor of ever larger specific grants, nor are they in favor of relatively string-less revenue sharing. One interesting expression of this somewhat vague solution occurs in *The Report of the President's Task Force on Model Cities:*

> Any 'solution' to the fundamental problems of the large cities will have to be found largely in the suburban fringes, the area where most of the growth is taking place. The key measures will be ones that hasten the movement of the poor and the black out of the inner city slums and semi-slums to places where jobs and other opportunities are relatively good.[8]

Although certain large specialized grants may be of value in a few cases, it is the writer's opinion that the first approach noted above will not prove much more fruitful in the future than it has in the past, even if the amounts of money were vastly increased.

Probably a judicious combination of the second and third approaches would be best. Cities need the chance, through block grants or shared revenue, to make their own decisions. At the same time, the Federal government should take any steps which will help the poor—white and black—to find a better economic and social life outside the slum areas. As we have noted, productive uses for the vacated areas can always be found, but should not be found at the expense of the present residents.

Finally, important as is a better federal-city working relationship, there must be no effect of by-passing the states which not only have important legal authority but may also be financially and administratively helpful partners in the task of solving urban problems.

STATE HELP—WAKING OUT OF LETHARGY

Diverse State Policies

We have stressed before, and we shall continue to stress, that state participation in solving urban problems is indispensable. However, one of the gravest difficulties faced by the student of "state policy toward cities" is the immense diversity among the states. Generalizations have the unhappy experience of running head-on into innumerable exceptions.

For instance, theoretically, state governments have complete control over the establishment, operation, and financing of local units. The sole federal intervention in this area comes under the Fourteenth Amendment and various judicial decisions concerning segregation and civil rights. However, many state constitutions impose limits on both the legislative and executive branches in certain areas affecting urban affairs, and thus impede any reasonable over-all state policy.

By rigidly prescribing the form of county government and requiring election of certain county officials, state constitutions may increase the difficulties of large metropolitan areas which, as we have noted earlier, often include more than one county. Many state constitutions set limits on taxation by local units. The constitutional specifications on the length of legislative sessions have an important, although indirect, effect on the problem-solving capacities of the state legislature. When it is remembered that the bulk of regulations governing such "every-day" matters as crime, estates, divorce, child care, family life, business activities, are formulated at the state level, it is obvious that an excessively short session leaves no time for a thorough exhaustive study of various proposals. Finally, the "long ballot" so divides administrative responsibility that strong executive leadership is impossible. Since state constitutions vary widely, generalizations must be tentative.

The quality of administration personnel also varies widely. Almost all the larger states have fairly well established civil service systems. Probably, on an *average,* state civil servants are less well-paid, less well-educated, and less efficient than federal civil servants, but this is not true in states like New York, California, and Wisconsin, where both line and staff employees compare very favorably with their federal counterparts.

The concept of "corrupt" state legislatures is somewhat outdated if one means selling a vote for a check. It is probably true that local "lobbying" (sometimes for the purest of causes) can put more pressure on a representative of a small area than on a representative of a larger one. Service in the state legislature has always been more prestigious in rural sections, and there is some question as to whether the one-man, one-vote reapportionment may not have replaced the bumbling county squire with the by-no-means bumbling urban representative. Later we shall discuss how little the reapportionment contributed to the improvement of urban areas.

It is also impossible to generalize about the extent to which states have subsidized local budgets. As we shall discuss more fully later, states carry most of the cost of higher education, but Hawaii in 1966 had assumed 100% of local school costs while New Hampshire had assumed less than 10%. Hawaii paid 70.4% of all state *and local* general expenditures; Alaska, 66.8%. In contrast, New Jersey paid only 24.1% and New York only 22.9% of these general expenditures. Even these figures are not strictly comparable, because some states make special grants for certain local functions.

On the whole, state highway departments have close contact with county road departments and with city street departments. Local school districts, which prepare students for state supported colleges, receive many types of aid from state departments of public instruction. There is usually less cooperation on the law enforcement level, largely because most states lack a comprehensive and well-organized state police agency.

At this point, it might be relevant to comment on the part which the federal government has played in further confusing the state-local relationships. The Department of Agriculture has customarily funneled its grants through the state governments or through state colleges. On the other hand, Housing and Urban Development grants are usually made directly to cities, by-passing the state administrative and legislative mechanism. This latter federal decision may be more important than a "rurally-oriented" legislature in divorcing urban problems from state governmental attention.

Weaknesses of the States

This section could be endless—as could any discussion of the weaknesses of the Federal government or the weaknesses of local government! We shall try to concentrate on a few general problems which seem peculiar to the state level.

It was long fashionable to blame the failure of state governments to meet urban problems on mis-apportionment. It is quite true that rural areas were often over-represented. In California, two small mountain counties with a total population of a few thousand sent to the state legislature a state senator who had a vote equal to the vote of the senator from Los Angeles County who represented 4,500,000—more people, incidentally, than are represented by most United States Senators. In 1962 and 1964, the Supreme Court in the cases of Baker vs. Carr and Reynolds vs. Sims decided that this mal-apportionment was unconstitutional and states were ordered to provide that both houses of the legislature be elected on a "one man-one vote" basis. Since these decisions were handed down, the appropriate changes have been made in all state constitutions and statutes.[1] Curiously enough, as A. James Reichley has shown, this reapportionment did not have material impact on the urban problems.[2] Liberal advocates of the reform had overlooked certain other factors. Of course, the massive movement of population out from the central city to the suburbs meant that, in spite of the new regulations, almost no big cities achieve control of their state legislatures. But there seems also some doubt as to whether the failure to cope with urban problems did indeed arise from the ignorance, the insensitivity, or the bias of rural lawmakers.[3] Deeper causes, not easily susceptible to treatment by judicial decisions or changes in voting procedure, may be involved.

Perhaps the most important factor is basically financial. States on the whole *do* contribute to localities a large proportion of their tax revenues, but they simply do not have the fiscal surpluses to expand their support of the ever-growing and exceedingly complex urban needs. It must be remembered that the states per se have important and expensive governmental responsibilities. Most states carry the largest part of the cost of public higher education within their boundaries—a system of higher education which, despite its many faults, is the best supported and most extensive in the world. Most states meet the entire expenses of long-term correctional institutions and of long-term care of the mentally ill. Although there is, of course, much federal assistance, state budgets include enormous sums for highway construction. Usually, substantial amounts are allocated to public school systems. Approximately a third of all welfare costs are borne by the state governments. These are "traditional" state functions which continue to be performed—with varying levels of competency, to be sure, but still performed. It will be noted that many states do, in addition, support various municipal responsibilities. The question is: are state resources adequate to add further subsidy to urban projects?

Nowhere is it more necessary to caution against generalizations than in the field of state finances. In the United States as a whole, the chief state sources of revenue in order of decreasing yield are: general sales taxes, selective sales taxes (such as alcoholic beverages, tobacco, motor fuels, etc.), individual income, and corporation net income.[4] However, the diversity is enormous. It is as easy as it is accurate to cite statistics showing that certain states have neglected possible tax sources and that others have consciously used tax "gimmicks" in competition with other states. But it is less easy to assert moralistically that all of the aberrations of state financing are due to malevolent influences.

Let us take, for example, the state income tax. Forty-two states now impose such taxes. Most of these are relatively modest because, while the taxpayer is permitted a 100% "deduction" of his state tax from his total income, he is not allowed a "credit" against his federal tax for taxes paid to the state. (This is, at times, a very costly distinction.) At the current high federal income tax rate, each state naturally hesitates to burden its own citizens with a levy substantially above that of other states. For some time, Florida actually advertised its freedom from income and inheritance taxes as an inducement to wealthy prospective residents, and Nevada has attracted affluent Californians by its lack of an income tax and by many other convenient "tax advantages." Admittedly, the situations seem at times somewhat whimsical: New Jersey has a corporation income tax, but no individual income tax for New Jersey residents. It does, however, receive $14.5 million from New York residents who derive income from New Jersey sources!

Another clearly competitive ploy used by thirty-two states relates to bonds. Tax-free bonds are permitted to build industrial sites in the hope of attracting job-producing and revenue-producing out-of-state capital.[5]

Probably the national government could eliminate much of this inter-state diversity by a thoughtful program which permitted full credit against federal tax liability for taxes paid to a state, but it should be admitted that the problem is a complex one.

Most state constitutions were drafted long before the Federal government seemed much more than an agency for defense and diplomatic relations. It has been estimated that as of 1900, local taxing units received and disbursed more than the combined total of *all* federal and state fiscal resources combined. These state constitutional conventions, therefore, totally unimpressed by the Federal government, chiefly desired to limit the taxing, borrowing, and administrative powers which they would allocate to the state. As a result, as we have noted before, they have set arbitrary time limits on legislative sessions and arbitrary salary limits on legislators. They set arbitrary debt limits. They prescribe the "long ballot," that is, separate election of the various state officers who presumably are to work cooperatively with the governor. (As if several cabinet members in the Presi-

dential Cabinet were to be separately elected.) Sometimes the
constitutional requirements lead to administrative chaos, sometimes to reasonable administrative compromise. In any event,
one should question whether the "will of the people" is well
served when the administration becomes a conglomerate of divergent political views. Former Governor Sanford points out that
in Utah, the governor is merely one of a troika, since all major
expenditure decisions must be made in conjunction with two
other separately elected officials.[6] Control over all Oregon state
institutions is vested in a Board composed of separately elected
governor, secretary of state, and treasurer. New Hampshire has
a constitutionally elected separate "Council of Five" which can
veto certain gubernatorial decisions and must approve all gubernatorial appointments. In Florida, six other elected officials
share executive authority with the governor. Obviously in such
cases the governor is handicapped in developing or implement-
ing any over-all policies.

A third problem is related to relatively recent changes in the
nature of the "metropolitan area" which is now composed of core
city and suburbs. For obvious political and sociological reasons,
the dominant urban party has been the party most identified
with "machines." While, as we have noted before, a large part
of the blatant corruption has been cleared up, it is still true that
liberal reformers who come to the state legislature to plead some
urgent urban need may find themselves accompanied by, or at
least supported by, legislators with "machine" connections. It
has been easy for those who are indifferent to, if not opposed to,
large scale urban programs to organize suburban and rural votes
against "machine politicians."[7] From a purely practical standpoint, the sincere advocate of urban reform should identify himself more with suburbia, should try to show that "urban" problems spill over into the surrounding area, that there is no neat
dividing line, for instance, between the District of Columbia and
Chevy Chase. Certainly suburban leaders need to be educated,
but so also do urban leaders. Only when the latter realize that
their natural allies are the former, can they together make an
impact on the state legislature.

What the States Have Done

We have been looking chiefly at the debit side of state contributions to solution of urban problems, but there are some credits to be chalked up.

Unfortunately, precise figures on state grants-in-aid to localities are not so readily available as are figures on federal grants.[8] States now turn over, under varying conditions, $20 billion to local units, while the Federal government turns over $28 billion to "states and localities," much of which (in one way or another) is channelled to local units or local services. It should be noted that the states are, on an over-all average, giving to localities almost 50% of their total tax revenues (total state revenues were $42 billion in 1969). The Federal government is giving to state/local units about one-seventh of its tax income. Over half of the state grants are to local school districts. Welfare grants are a weak second. Street-highway projects are third. There are many minor grants, several on the "pass-through" basis: namely, federal grants which are state administered but designed for local use. On the whole, state grants to localities tend to have less involved conditions than do federal grants to states for local use or federal grants directly to local units. State grants, like federal grants, are usually for specifically designated functions (and thus do not materially strengthen the local unit as a governmental entity), but they usually do not, as do many federal grants, involve the establishment of special districts which introduce still another level to complicate local jurisdictional problems.

Belatedly, the states have faced up to the complexity of the "metropolitan problem." More and more they are turning from a few re-allocated funds, a few efforts at rationalization of local units, a few state-level experts in advisory capacities, to large-scale programs to assist the cities. Since 1968, twenty states have instituted state departments for urban planning and development.[9] A few examples are outstanding. New Jersey has a new Department of Community Affairs. It has mass-transit programs, urban renewal programs, and war-on-poverty programs, with a $26 million appropriation and a bonding authorization of $25 million per year. It also created in 1969 a Hackensack Meadowlands Development Commission with authority for much physical improvement in the area. Pennsylvania established in 1966 a cabinet-level "Department of Community Affairs." It too included mass transit, war-on-poverty, and urban renewal projects with $47.3 million in appropriations for 1969. New York set up an "Urban Development Corporation" in 1968. Its powers included housing construction, urban renewal, commercial and industrial development. Kolesar estimates that with its own and private financial backing it could support $5 billion of physical redevelopment. Reilly and Schuman believe that this kind of state corporation may be a way of getting blacks out of the central city ghettos into appropriate housing somewhere in the suburbs.[10] It may be that New York and New Jersey, both geographically small and very populous, are not providing the solutions appropriate for Texas and Alaska, but it is possible that each state may best cope with its own specific urban problems. A recent study of the relation between state highway construction and urban situations in Maryland and Washington shows that the Governor's office had an active role in establishing the highway systems. As the article comments, governors of predominantly urban states tend to concern themselves with the impact of state-wide programs on urban areas.[11]

Just as the most ardent advocate of free enterprise should desire a governmentally established legal framework within which free enterprise can function, so the most ardent supporter of local self-government should want the states to establish a workable framework of local governmental units.

While most states have been lamentably backward in this matter, some have introduced thoughtful measures. Arizona now has a law which prohibits new governmental incorporations within six miles of an existing city—a regulation which does not solve pre-existing metropolitan problems but does prevent further complications. Virginia has for decades prescribed that a municipality may annex adjoining territory by a court proceeding—a system which permits careful review of evidence for annexation and is much superior to the customary state laws which require favorable popular votes of both annexing and annexed areas. California has established county-wide municipal boundary commissions to arbitrate problems between municipalities. Larger school districts have in several states been organized both to economize on basic services and to permit development of larger-area schools for a wide range of "specialized" groups—those desiring vocational education, those physically handicapped, those emotionally disturbed, those intellectually exceptional on the "superior" level, and those intellectually exceptional on the "retarded" level. No small school district could possibly fund all of these services.

State Legislative Responsibilities

The Advisory Commission on Intergovernmental Relations, which was set up by the executive branch of the federal government in 1959 and which includes both state and local officials, has made a far more extensive study of such relationships than any other body. The following recommendations, paraphrased by this author for purposes of brevity, represent the best program thus far advanced for federal and state assistance in solving the financial aspects of the urban problem.[12]

1. The states should assume substantially all responsibility for financing public education.
2. The national government should assume full financial responsibility for public assistance (including general assistance and medicare).
3. States should compensate cities for the overburden of some municipalities in the absence of substantial state support for schools.
4. States should equalize more in giving state aid for health and hospital programs.
5. Federal aid to highways should be revamped to place more attention on state systems, including urban transportation.
6. States should develop a mass transportation plan and give assistance to metropolitan areas in this field.
7. States should rebalance their highway resources to give a better break to the cities.

8. State constitutions should be amended to allow greater flexibility of use of transportation funds.
9. Each state should study its state-aid plan and review and evaluate it carefully.
10. Each state should establish criteria for assessing the viability of local governments so that it will not be supporting unworkable units. Some state agency should have the power, subject to court review, to dissolve or consolidate local governmental units within metropolitan areas.
11. Each state should use performance reporting in studying its categorical grants-in-aid.
12. State grant-in-aid legislation should require conformance to local, regional, and state-wide plans.

In a separate document, the Commission adds to the above recommendations 1. and 2. (that the Federal government should assume all financial responsibility for welfare and the states substantially all support of public education) a hearty endorsement for some plan of sharing federal revenue with states and localities.[13] These three proposals have many advantages. Welfare has always been a "national" problem, since people move freely from state to state, but the recent Supreme Court decision which eliminates residence requirements for welfare benefits immeasurably increases federal responsibility in this field. It is equally clear that education has inter-area significance. The school children of x county will in all probability be the workers and the voters of y or z county, and the quality of their education is of more than narrowly local interest. Revenue-sharing is, at this writing, still a controversial topic, but it seems inevitable that it will be adopted in some form or other, when one remembers the minimal tax sources of some areas, the immense diversity even among state tax potentialities, and the broad base of federal resources.

Most of the other recommendations are highly desirable also, as they would bring state governments more actively into cooperation in solving urban problems and would require more rational planning and coordination of state grants to localities.

The difficulty with such a multi-faceted program as that advocated by the Advisory Commission is obvious: it is very hard to put into effect, simply because it necessitates a delicate dovetailing of many complicated elements. Federal and state governments would have to agree—a very difficult task.

On the state level, there are many problems. Many state legislators sincerely feel that, apart from the fiscal problems, states should not assume all of the cost of public education with the necessarily attendant state supervision; that there should continue to be a strong local stake in what they deem an important local function. Moreover, as we have noted above, states are not likely to view with much enthusiasm joint state-urban efforts so long as many "urban" representatives continue in conflict not only with the decreasingly important rural legislators but also with the increasingly important suburban legislators with whom they should be working for the general metropolitan good. While the states should make heavier contributions to such services as education, and mass transportation, many of them have genuine fiscal problems themselves. As we shall note later, the federal government could do much to encourage a closer state-urban relationship but it could also work out some practicable program of financial assistance.

State Involvement in Urban Affairs

In general, there is an urgent need for more state involvement in urban problems. But there is also a need to assess realistically how much the states could do independently and how much is contingent on federal policies.

At the state level there are three major improvements probably which could be initiated.

1. Through its legal control of the local taxing power, the state could enable local governments to expand their tax bases. Current laws often preclude quite wealthy local units from utilizing possible sources. At the same time, most states should pass on more of their tax proceeds to localities. All states do make some grants to local units, but there has not been sufficient attention to the "equalizing" principle because tax controls and grants have often worked at cross purposes.

2. Through its legal control over forms of local government, the state could reduce the number of over-lapping local governmental areas, and thus make local units more efficient and less expensive. In some cases, constitutional provisions are a handicap, but in many cases the state legislature has merely been indifferent.

3. Most states could absorb into their budgets a small amount of money to provide advisory services which could serve as "clearing houses"—transmitting mutually helpful information and suggestions between states and their local units.

At the Federal level, the Government could do much, and has done lamentably little, to facilitate state-urban cooperation.

1. Public housing, for example, is one field in which Washington has had what might be called an "actively negative" impact. When the national grants to public housing started in the 1930's, the national administration had a profound distrust of state governments. Only enabling legislation was sought, and the states were completely by-passed to the great disadvantage of the entire program. In fact, at times, even existing local governments were ignored, and federal administrators dealt directly with federally established local housing authorities.

A few states have supported public housing on their own. In New York, for instance, there are federally financed and state financed projects side by side. Generally, however, the national policy has discouraged state action in this field—a situation deprecated by former Governor Sanford. As he comments: "More states should be involved directly in housing problems. Why not involve them and call upon them for a positive contribution? Perhaps the states are in the best position to support, coordinate, and lead in zoning, planning land use, developing low-cost housing, preventing slums, and working toward adequate housing."[14]

2. If the national government had, in housing as well as in many other fields, made grants to states to set up agencies to assist local units, and also made grants to states conditional upon the latter putting up some money for most urgent urban needs, the states could have begun playing a constructive role two decades ago. Why has Congress been so backward? At least three reasons may be suggested.

It should be noted that state governments have long been the targets of often virulent criticism by political scientists, reform journalists, and many outstanding public figures. It is true that the state level has not always performed well and that many improvements were needed. However, the almost entirely destructive nature of the approach failed to take into account the many important functions which are constitutionally served by the states, and the hard reality that, in many fields, urban problems simply cannot be solved without state cooperation. Another factor is that Congress has tended in the area of inter-governmental relations to rely upon a variety of specialized associations, specialized bureaus, and specialized committees which have not even tried to think about urban problems in a broad context. And, finally, there has not been until very recently a thoughtful mechanism for establishing a sound national policy towards state-local relations. The Advisory Committee on Inter-governmental Relations has for some years made important reports, but it is not a policy-setting body.

Future Possibilities

1. A useful device which could be expanded is a system whereby states would be asked to "buy-in" to federal grants to localities, that is, supply a share of the money needed to match a federal grant. There has been a disinclination to make this a strict federal requirement, since, if a state failed to comply, the urban government might lose much needed funds. In at least one recent case—the Omnibus Crime Control Act of 1970—Congress did require the state government to pay one quarter of the non-federal portion of grants. In the instance of this relatively small subsidy, the federal provision is not likely to hold up the grant, but it might where larger sums were involved. Major grants in the welfare field are almost always channelled through the states, since local units could not meet the matching provisions themselves. The funds are "passed through" to localities after state approval of local programs.

The Advisory Commission on Intergovernmental Relations has recommended "buying-in" on a voluntary basis.[15] Some similar type of state participation in federal grants to localities has been urged by the Kestenbaum Commission, the National Governors' Conference, a Task Force of the Urban Coalition, and the Council of State Governments.[16]

Stenberg, in a careful study of "buying-in" by New York State on Aviation Grants, concludes that the system definitely results in more flexible cost-sharing arrangements, expanded local program scope, and reduced local costs. To a lesser extent, it promotes state-local planning coordination and general state-local cooperation.[17]

2. Fortunately, there are a few other signs of increased willingness to recognize the importance of the states. Certainly, President Nixon's revenue-sharing plan would not only strengthen the states financially but would also permit them to be of more assistance to localities. The Model Cities program included cooperation with some state governments. The Omnibus Crime Control and Safe Streets Act of 1968, already mentioned, was another effort to tie in the states to urban problems.

3. In addition to these specific fields of legislation, there is probably need for some over-all agency within the Federal government to study and encourage further progress. Senator Muskie has suggested a National Intergovernmental Affairs Council. John Gardner, as Secretary of Health, Education, and Welfare, also recognized the need for some focal center for the revitalization of state governments. Former Governor Sanford has recommended that all bills involving intergovernmental relations be submitted to the Government Operations Committee of each House of Congress.[18] The writer believes that in addition to the excellent Advisory Committee on Intergovernmental Relations, there should be a larger unit in the Office of Management and Budget working on this problem.

In the past, the states have not sufficiently involved themselves with urban problems—in part because of their own financial difficulties and in part because of constitutional restrictions. They do, however, have much legal authority to introduce changes, and they are showing an increasing awareness of their responsibility. Finally, the federal government, which long functioned almost as an enemy of state governments, is now tending to encourage a really concerted federal-state-local approach to the many difficulties which do indeed overlap rigid jurisdictional lines.

URBAN SELF-HELP—
FINANCIAL ASPECTS

6 ★ ★ ★

Before discussing existing tax sources and possible additional ones, it should be noted that the very serious fiscal condition of many large cities is in part due to factors over which they have no control. In the first place, obviously, welfare, education, policing, fire control, public works, all cost more in the central city, but the most productive human "tax resources" largely reside in the suburbs. In the second place, frequently federal and state laws impose certain expenditures on the city governments. Mayor Lindsay of New York testified to the Congressional Joint Economic Committee on January 23, 1971, that his city must pay $600 million a year for a welfare program the terms of which were all dictated in Albany and Washington. He might have added that in Washington, at least, none of the persons who drafted those terms had any clear impression of their effect on any given municipal budget.

The General Property Tax

Still the major source of local revenue is the general property tax. It supplies over half of the total—almost $30 billion in 1968–1969. It will probably continue to be a fiscal mainstay, but it has conspicuous limitations and disadvantages.

Since the tax must legally be based on assessed valuation, and since there are obvious limits to the percentage of valuation which can be levied as a tax, it yields less revenue in poor areas than in wealthy ones. Thirty years ago big cities were viewed as centers of wealth. Financial equalization laws (chiefly state grants to school districts) were designed to take taxes away from the prosperous city and to give larger grants to the poorer rural areas. Since that time, we have noted, the more affluent citizens have on the whole left the central city, and the poor and the black, lacking alternative home sites, have moved in. Property values have declined relative to those in other areas. At the same time governmental costs have mounted astronomically. There are not only more children to educate per $10,000 of assessed valuation; there are also more children who need special educational services. And, as was stated above, welfare costs are enormously larger than in suburbs, and usually police and fire protection must be more extensive.

We all know examples of this imbalance between property tax revenues and governmental needs. The Newtons and Brookline maintain a high level of local services, while Boston constantly declines. The North Lake Shore suburbs like Winnetka and Wilmette have better schools and more effective law enforcement than does Chicago. The difference between Beverly Hills or San Marino and Watts or Willowbrook is notorious well beyond the confines of Southern California.

It is time to face up to the fact that poorer cities simply are unable to render proper governmental services on the revenue available in large part from the general property tax. Perhaps the most striking example of this is the working class "dormitory city." With no industry to tax, and with only the most modest homes whose assessed valuation is—quite reasonably—low, the city tax income is totally inadequate. It is true that salaries of teachers, policemen, firemen, and other "public servants" may seem disgraceful, but the city is not to blame. With some qualifications to be noted later in this chapter, these cities are genuinely doing the best they can to meet ends which are beyond their means.

Most of the previous points are fairly obvious. There is one somewhat more complicated point which might be noted. In many jurisdictions, the "property" tax is laid more heavily on the building than on the land. As Henry George insisted almost a century ago in *Progress and Poverty,* this tends to discourage construction or large investment in maintenance or reconstruction. No one today seriously advocates his "single tax" on land, but a number of people are wondering if land should not be taxed more heavily than improvements. However, in most states, constitutional amendments would be needed to permit heavier taxation of land. If *land* were taxed more heavily, there would be an incentive to improve the buildings situated on that land. In some cases, a land tax might result in better utilization of space, better buildings, and more local revenue.

Other Tax Sources

As we have just indicated, cities cannot increase the property tax rates on assessed valuation of structures without discouraging home ownership, urban improvement, or new construction. Some large cities like Boston and Milwaukee seem already to have reached the point where major new construction is very difficult.

On the whole, the quest for other tax sources has been disappointing:

1. Most cities have some revenue from license fees on businesses and professions. However, some states set limits on the amount which can be prescribed, and even when this is not the case, it is only obvious common sense not to make such licenses burdensome.

2. A number of local governments have secured permission to levy municipal income taxes, especially on the commuter who makes his money downtown but lives in a wealthy low-tax suburb.[1] Over 3,500 local jurisdictions use this tax—3,458 of them located in Ohio and Pennsylvania. The rate most frequently specified is 1%, but usually when the tax is applied to non-residents, the rate is lower. Although most of the governmental units experimenting with this source are quite small, it has, surprisingly, yielded over 70% of the tax income for such significant Ohio cities as Canton, Columbus, Springfield, and Youngstown.[2]

The disadvantage lies in adding to the already heavy combination of income taxes imposed by the federal government and most states. Moreover, the commuter may be liable at his place of residence and at his place of work. At certain levels, this might reduce the incentive—if not to work, at least to seek advancement.

A better solution to the problem of the commuter is to charge him for the costs which his travel and presence devolve upon the city during the work week. There is no reason why the dweller in the central city, whose income is usually lower than that of the suburbanite—should pay for the streets, roads, traffic police, signals used by the latter in going from and to his expensive home. Some appropriate charge for these and other services is in order. One simple and effective way of arranging this would be collection of a substantial daily fee for every car coming into the downtown.

3. In nineteen states, local units are authorized to add a small percentage (ranging from ¼% to 3%) to the state sales tax. The yield may be very substantial, especially to the city with a well-established shopping center. Therein, of course, lies the inequity. The surrounding cities may, through their citizens, be contributing special help to a commercial rival.

Service Charges

Many cities have recently supplemented revenues by charging for services rendered. Municipal water departments have always sent bills—ones sometimes inadequate to cover costs, but still bills. There seems no reason why a city should not charge for garbage collection, rubbish collection, even sewage service; although probably exceptions should be worked out to cover cases of real poverty. In any event, as state laws permit, municipalities are increasingly using this means to add to revenues, and in 1968–69, $8 billion out of a total of $72 billion local revenue came from such sources.

Some entrance charges for art, historical, and industrial museums now exist, and considerable sentiment is developing in favor of expanding the custom. As American tourists know, most European museums and even some noteworthy churches have fees to help pay operating costs, and Great Britain, which long resisted the practice, is now adopting it.[3] With the heavy pressure on local governments for such essential functions as welfare,

education, and policing, it may be impossible to provide free
these other services. At least one well-known professor has
seriously advocated a small charge for the use of local parks,
on the theory that a park is a recreational opportunity which
will be more appreciated and better used if not completely
free.

Related to this topic of justifiable service charges is the question of tuition for attendance at city universities. Almost all
states now charge tuition—very substantial amounts in some
cases although, of course, less than independent institutions. It
is curious to note that the State University of New York charges
several hundred dollars a year, but the City University of New
York, which receives a substantial state subsidy, is entirely
free! On the other hand, municipal universities elsewhere
collected in 1968–69 some $264 million to assist with their ex-
penses.

To the writer, the general principle is perfectly clear. No student who wants, and will work for, a higher education should be
deprived on financial grounds. Adequate scholarship funds
should always be set up. On the other hand, there is no reason
why a well-to-do student should be educated at public expense
by a city hard pressed to meet many desperate needs.

Federal and State Grants—or Revenue Sharing

In the final analysis, no possible combination of new local
taxes and service charges will make much impact on central city
budgets. The most promising source of funds is still federal and
state grants or revenue sharing. The re-allocation suggested by
the Advisory Commission—federal government, all welfare;
state government, all education; some revenue-sharing with local units—would probably be the best solution. But when we
realize that in 1968–1969 only $44 billion was raised by local
resources, while state grants provided $24 billion and direct fed-
eral grants $2¼ billion, we can see that the subsidy is imperative
under some form or other. Currently, the chief problem with the

grants is that they are too numerous, too specific, and almost totally uncoordinated. Certainly, revenue sharing has many advantages, but functional block grants containing fewer restrictions are properly urged by associations of cities and other groups interested in the solution of urban problems.

A frequent topic of discussion is the extent to which acceptance of state or federal grants weakens "local control"—on the general theory that "he who pays the piper calls the tune." On this point several comments could be made.

1. Insofar as possible, cities should be allowed and encouraged to develop their own revenue sources and thus to maintain or even expand their area of financial autonomy. However, we have seen, complete local autonomy in this sense is no longer a possibility. There seems little reason to doubt that municipal control of personnel or of limited policy-making can survive if effective representatives of cities and other local units carefully watch the legislation and the administrative regulations and steadfastly oppose overly-restrictive provisions.

2. It must be remembered that states have—and should have—the power to control local units by legislation—whether or not attached to grants. Public education, for instance, has long been subject to state laws on teacher certification, curriculum, and a number of other school matters not necessarily tied to financial aid. Similarly, the Supreme Court, and not state or federal subsidies, is responsible for enforcement of integration, busing, and other aspects of pupil placement.

3. Finally, federal and state governments do not want, and certainly do not have time for, any very detailed supervision. For instance, the drive for local autonomy in New York's black school districts is primarily concerned with the power to hire or retain individual teachers. This is a "control" which federal or state commissioners could not possibly physically exert and one which, in view of the administrative headaches involved, they could not possibly desire!

New York City Finances—an Example

Both because New York is the largest and presumably wealthiest city in the country and because its financial problems have been more thoroughly studied than those of other cities, this section will be devoted to a somewhat detailed summary of its situation. The chief sources are articles by David Bernstein and by Dick Netzer, although other material has been consulted.[4]

According to Bernstein, the Mayor's budget for 1969–1970 was $6.6 billion, 10% above the budget adopted for the previous year. For five years, the budget has been increasing at a rate of $580 million a year—a rate of increase which had no parallel in the preceding three decades. It was several times greater than the increase in the Consumer Price Index, twice the rise of the Gross National Product. In the years 1957–1965, expenditures in New York had risen 7% a year; those in other large cities, 5.5% a year.

Two major factors accounted for 70% of the recent increases: rising salaries and benefits of city employees, and an enormously larger welfare budget, including medical assistance. In 1971, Mayor Lindsay "rejected" the still rising welfare budget as beyond the city's ability to handle. (It is true that in many other large cities, some responsibility for welfare is borne by other units of government.)

Changing aspects of city revenues were also studied by Bernstein. Real estate taxes had been increasing, but were becoming a smaller fraction of the total budget (47% in 1958–1959; 29% in 1968–1969). The estimated 1969–1970 yield was $1,800 million. The next largest resource was a sales tax which produced $468 million. Business income tax, personal income tax, stock transfer tax, and other miscellaneous charges helped to bring the city's own income (exclusive of federal and state aid) up to $3,721,000 in 1969–1970. Bernstein believes that since the city is already a high "tax island" there would be grave difficulties in trying to raise the rates of any of these taxes, and that there is little chance that the *city* can raise the extra quarter of a billion dollars still needed to balance the budget.

In the decade 1959–1969, state aid has grown from 18% to 27% of the municipal budget; federal aid from 5% to 15%. In 1968–1969, state aid amounted to $1,611 million, and federal aid to $892 million.

Working from the same basic figures, Netzer agrees on certain points with Bernstein but makes certain other observations. He finds evidence of a tendency to put too many items in the Capital Budget which is partly financed by borrowing. While he feels that the city's income from the general property tax will be "less buoyant" in the next few years because of the recent slowdown in housing activities, he thinks that more income will be derived from its net income tax on businesses and progressive personal income tax on residents. Moreover, he recommends that New York might well reconsider its policy of a lower tax on land than on buildings, citing Henry George's contention that government should tax the unearned increment in land values more heavily. As a result of Mayor Lindsay's reforms, the city has finally started to make more nearly adequate water and sewer charges, and this should be of help in the future. Netzer notes, as we mentioned earlier, that the City University, unlike most state universities, still requires no tuition while it has enormously expanded all of its programs. And, finally, he comments that the *increase* in state aid which had certainly been steadily climbing for a decade, came to a "screeching halt" in the 1969 Legislature.

On the major components of the larger expenditures Netzer agrees with Bernstein: public assistance grants and health grants have expanded spectacularly, and employee compensation has risen much more sharply in New York City than elsewhere. While he rejects the frequently made assertion that city employees are doing less work for more pay than formerly, the outside observer might question the justice of New York asking for assistance from other units of government to subsidize the very high compensation levels forced on the city by its employee unions.

Netzer concludes: "All this is to argue that if New York City seems ungovernable, it is not because of the City's great size, but because the City's government is too big in the sense that it does too many things." Some of its functions should be turned over to other levels of government.

Still another appraisal of expenditures in New York is given in a report of the Association of the Bar of the City of New York issued in 1970. It lists an impressive array of expensive improvements in the past decade: 3,700 new police patrolmen; treatment centers for drug addicts; higher welfare payments; greatly increased use of hospitals; lower student-teacher ratio; and smaller class size in public schools; increase in fire fighting personnel and equipment; improved and expanded snow and trash removal facilities. "Yet," to quote the report, "these increases have not produced any parallel increase in satisfaction with the quality of life in New York City for most New Yorkers. One explanation is that the need for many services is rising even faster than the increase in the level of the services provided."

Bernstein makes much the same point. New York has "more people, more businesses, more jobs, and more income than any other city; but also more poor people, bigger slums, worse labor problems, and higher city costs and taxes." He might have added that it costs more to do everything in New York City.

A comparison of these three analyses leaves the writer with the conclusion that New York City does need help, although not so desperately as some New York City authorities contend. But its example has instructive implications for other cities. In spite of high and variegated city taxes, and in spite of enormous federal and state aid, the costs outrun the available revenue. The "plight of the cities" is by no means imaginary.

Saving Funds Through Efficiency

It is undoubtedly true that many large cities could save money through better administrative policies, and so the question might validly be raised whether municipal inefficiency should be subsidized by state and federal grants. Unfortunately, however, simple solutions to complicated problems are difficult to find.

The District of Columbia school system is an interesting example. *The Washington Post,* a newspaper which customarily supports increased governmental expenditures, ran an article entitled "D.C. Schools: Is Money the Answer?" [5] According to the article, Washington was spending more money per pupil than all but two of its (largely wealthy) suburbs, and its teacher salaries averaged higher than all but one suburban neighbor. It is no particular secret that the District school system is not considered a very effective one. It is clear that many of the larger expenditures were ones that may be justifiable for a predominantly black and predominantly poor area. The school lunch program is necessarily more extensive, and although food is furnished by the federal government, cost of preparation and service is borne by the school district. More reading specialists are essential, and more gym, art, and music teachers probably desirable. Teachers, union officials, and administrators unanimously agree that more funds are needed, as indeed do most other citizens. On the other hand, what seemed to be an excellent plan for improving education in the basic skills was, if not "rejected," certainly neglected. Some skepticism as to whether money *alone* is the answer can be understood.

The salaries of New York City employees, already mentioned, are another questionable source of expense.

On the other hand, central city populations have certain basic needs which must be met, no matter how inefficient their governments. City governments should be encouraged and assisted in the task of becoming more efficient. A municipal corporation should be subject to many of the financial restraints that apply to any other corporation. It must see that its revenues and expenditures are properly accounted for; it must develop sound financial plans for both capital and current purposes; it cannot expect to meet every demand of employee unions without expecting revolt from taxpayers against unlimited tax increases. But, in the last analysis, if these reasonable requirements are met and if the citizens—especially the minority groups—are well served, then the rest of the state or of the country should help the cities find financial means to solve their problems.

7 ★ ★ ★

URBAN SELF-HELP:
POLITICAL AND
ADMINISTRATIVE IMPROVEMENT

Before considering the various specific ways in which localities could help themselves in the solution of their problems, a few political observations seem in order.

Whereas it would be idle to contend that cities do not need financial assistance from federal and state levels and encouragement in devising more efficient mechanisms, it is also true that many of the past and present difficulties must be squarely met by the local units themselves. Not the least of these is pressure from various groups which, in one form or another, are inimical to the general well-being of the community. Fortunately, the old-fashioned political machine survives in very few places. At one time, at least some of their corruption and low personnel standards could be forgiven because machines did perform some useful function in making new ethnic groups feel "noticed"—not completely awash in a strange environment. But these ethnic groups are now better educated, less narrowly ethnic in political thought, and more independent. There is no longer a place for the ward boss in the complexities of modern city politics. And, as we have pointed out elsewhere, reformers made a sad mistake in accepting such assistance when assistance was never given in securing local reform.

Another source of danger in certain cities has been the effort of organized crime to associate itself closely with the political mechanism. Parts of New York, New Jersey, Connecticut, and other states have suffered from this, and unquestionably at least one major city added to its already overwhelming social and economic problems the burden of a mayor known to have questionable connections.

Of course of a different sort but still potentially damaging to over-all fiscal or administrative reforms is the pressure of strong employee unions. They possess sufficient political power to have real impact on mayors and governors—a power often exerted for narrowly selfish ends.

A second general comment is that, within a governmental structure, administrative problems cannot always be solved solely on the basis of maximum efficiency. Some attention must be paid to "political" elements, or popular opinion, within the community. For instance, a strictly enforced police curfew might be welcome in a well-to-do area, while it would arouse deep antagonism in a crowded poorer area where neither spacious homes nor adequate gathering places compensate for lack of access to street life. Some citizens are willing and able to pay for parks and beautification projects; others are not. Even the degree of administrative cooperation possible between adjacent local units depends upon the mood of the citizens within these units. The goal of efficiency cannot ignore the question of "citizen participation" discussed more fully later.

Governing Metropolitan Areas

Certainly smaller cities, not close to large urban areas, have their problems, and many of the suggestions made in this chapter may be useful to them. However, major emphasis will be put on the metropolis, because that is where the most urgent needs lie.

Ideally, some efficient form of "metropolitan government," distinct from city, county, or special districts, should be devised; but it is not often that this will happen. It is usually supported by a few progressive citizens, civic and business organizations, and the metropolitan press. But it is also opposed by many groups. The suburban press and many suburban residents of limited viewpoint are likely to avoid embroilment in "inner-city" problems. Blacks often feel that they wield more power within the core city than they could in a broader area. Local officials feel that their own authority or even jobs would be endangered. Therefore, it is only practicable for the thoughtful reformer to seek out other methods of securing cooperative solutions.

Certain examples of such a "federal city" outside of the United States are familiar to political scientists. The County of London, England renders certain services to people who secure other governmental services from smaller "boroughs" within the county. The metropolitan system of Toronto, Canada handles water supply, sewage disposal, housing, education, arterial highways, metropolitan parks, some welfare services, and general planning. Within the United States, the Dade County–Miami unit, already referred to, operates as a metropolitan district. So also functions the County of Los Angeles for the numerous cities within its limits, although it is not usually included in such lists. It furnishes such county-wide services as tax assessment (for all but two cities), tax collection, air pollution control, county planning, and county roads. It provides complete governmental services to unincorporated areas, and contracts out services to some cities.

In the case of larger cities, the separate organization of city and county is only confusing. Certain very desirable consolidations have already been made. Nashville and Davidson County in Tennessee voted to consolidate in 1962. Baton Rouge and East Baton Rouge Parish, Louisiana, merged in 1947; Jacksonville and Duval County in Florida in 1967; Indianapolis and Marion County, Indiana in 1969. There was state consent but little state leadership in these mergers.[1]

It is certainly true that a rejuvenated county government can help greatly in the solution of metropolitan problems. A more flexible and effective county government is desirable, and, after all, in most states the urbanly-important functions of welfare are assigned to county government. In a case such as that of Los Angeles County which includes a number of cities and is well run, the results have been very good. However, this is not a universal solution. One county does not usually include the entire metropolitan area. Moreover, counties are frequently badly administered by a number of elected officers whose elected status is specified in the state constitutions or state law.

There have been a few annexations to large cities in recent decades by four Texas cities—Houston, Dallas, Fort Worth, and San Antonio—and by Oklahoma City. In Chapter Five, we mentioned Virginia's system of judicial settlement of annexation problems.

There would be no real objection to forcing local government reorganization by conditioning federal and state grants upon such consolidation. A similar procedure has been used to effect school district consolidation. But this, of course, is not a matter of *local* choice.

Some progress has been made through formal or informal agreements between cities, or between cities and counties. Inter-city or county-city arrangements for exchange of police or fire service in time of emergency are very frequent. In relatively well-governed areas like Southern California, such agreements are almost universal. The organization of cities in the San Francisco Bay area has a paid staff and clears a number of joint problems.

An expansion of the informal agreement idea can be found in what might be called semi-metropolitan governmental units. These are metropolitan districts which do not take over all urban functions, but do handle problems of traffic, of sewage, of water supply, of highway construction, of policing, of fire control— those matters which clearly extend beyond narrow "city limit" definition.

Where cities have not been able to organize such metropolitan districts, other means of meeting the problem have been tried. In the Boston area, where the state was long suspicious of the ability of Boston to govern itself, the *state* created a special district to furnish regional parks and to meet transportation problems.

But in a wide number of metropolitan areas, voluntary planning agencies have been formed by the cities, with representatives of each constituent city on the boards.

The most striking examples of local cooperation are the relatively recent Councils of Government, of which by 1971 there were probably more than a hundred. These are councils of elected officials who meet to discuss common problems. To date, there has been major emphasis on planning of physical development. An article on these Councils in the 1970 *Municipal Year-*

book indicates that they are successfully operating in such widely distributed metropolitan areas as Washington, D.C., Philadelphia, Des Moines, Iowa, San Francisco (Association of Bay Area Officials), Salem, Oregon (Mid-Willamette Valley), Seattle, Washington (Puget Sound).[2]

It should be noted that these Councils are still not much more than creatures of federal administrative planning. Major support has come from the federal government, which has given financial help for planning projects and administrative assistance through the 1966 Demonstration Cities and Metropolitan Development Act which provided that localities must consult with the Councils before securing federal grants for certain purposes. However, they do represent progress in inter-city planning, and they do illustrate also the constructive role the federal government can play.

The cross references between cities, counties, and school districts are legion. Schools employ school nurses, who must, however, work with the county health departments in many ways, especially in control of epidemics. School playgrounds should be available as part of the weekend and vacation resources of the city recreation departments. Municipal libraries are not only open to school children; they are also often expected to give special services to the pupils. Welfare children, with their sometimes special needs such as free lunch programs, attend city schools. Unfortunately, city police are often required nowadays in public school buildings.

All of these intricate relationships could be—although frequently are not—worked out satisfactorily by administrative consultation and agreement. However, integration or more formal joint planning could accomplish more. Arlington County, Virginia (which itself combines city and county functions) presents an example of what can be done. It has organized its recreation department, part of its police work, and some of its community activities on the basis of Junior High School districts, thus ensuring county-school district coordination.[3]

The "special district" has frequently been a complicating factor in effective coordination of local government. School districts have led the way in consolidation of districts too small to furnish proper educational services, and it is to be hoped that this trend will continue. However, other special districts continue to multiply, and some areas are seeking solutions. One answer might be to consolidate the special district into a more general unit. The "dependent district," often employed in California, is in part at least under county supervision. However, as has been mentioned several times, California counties and especially Los Angeles County, are fortunately large enough to handle metropolitan problems in most parts of that state. Another useful reform is to combine several single-purpose districts into multiple-purpose districts as in the Boston case. These changes must be supported by the state legislature, but action is far more likely when municipalities have already agreed on the goal.

Administrative Machinery

The administrative machinery of American cities has made substantial progress in the last half-century. In general, there are three major forms of municipal government: the mayor-council, the commission, and the council-manager. The commission form, an almost totally unworkable one in which each separately elected commissioner heads a city department and then sits with his rival department heads on a council, existed in only 6.4% of the cities over 5,000 and is practically non-existent in large cities.[4]

There is considerable controversy over the relative merits of the council-manager and the mayor-council forms. The former, strikingly close to the business corporation set-up, gives better coordination under one professional executive. The latter places more stress on the political leadership of the elected mayor. Political scientists sometimes conclude that the increasingly popular city manager form is most desirable for small cities, is clearly the best administered, and most democratically responsible, but that the greater political leadership possible under the mayor-council form is needed in larger places. This may be true. At any rate, answers to the 1970 *Municipal Yearbook* question-

naire show an increasing trend toward the council-manager
form. Of the over 5,000 cities which responded (not all, of course,
did respond) 43% had the council-manager form. The mayor-
council form is used in 80% of the cities over 500,000; in only 51%
of the cities under that population. These figures do not necessarily prove or disprove the political scientist's analysis. Certainly, larger cities tend to cling to the older mayor-council form,
but there is little evidence whether the 20% who do not have lost
in leadership strength.

Lineberry and Fowler have made an interesting "multiple correlation" statistical study of "reformed" cities (that is, council-
manager cities with non-partisan elections), mayor-council cities
with partisan elections, and mayor-council cities with non-partisan elections.[5] They found that the council-manager cities both
spend less and tax less than do mayor-council cities, but there
was no tax-expenditure correlation when comparing partisan
and non-partisan election examples within the mayor-council
group. They conclude that council-manager cities are less responsive to social and economic cleavages within their populations. However, the problem is very complex. It may be that the
council-manager cities tax less and spend less because they are
unresponsive to some genuine needs; it may be because they use
more service charges and are are more generally efficient in the
"business-like" sense. The writer is inclined to think that this
form of municipal government is on the whole preferable, but
that the professional executive managers may need more education in the sociological aspects of their responsibilities.

Examples of Administrative Initiative

Under both mayor and manager plan, there is in every city of
reasonable size a constant opportunity for administrative initiative and improvement. Some of these programs are of purely
local significance, but many can be widely adopted—or adapted
to differing situations. Police chiefs, fire chiefs, street departments, building inspectors, hospital administrators, welfare officials, and other groups have associations which have annual (or

more frequent) meetings to discuss common problems. It is most instructive to attend these meetings or to read the publications of the various groups. Listed below are a few of the significant achievements in various fields reported from all over the country.[6]

1. POLICE AND CRIME CONTROL   The District of Columbia has done an outstanding job in recruiting black officers. One factor may be large recruiting vans based on the edge of black districts.

St. Louis has a special "Mobile Reserve" to saturate heavy crime areas at the time of greatest criminal activity.

Similarly, New York City has added a fourth platoon which enables it to muster extra police strength during the high crime hours of 8 P.M. to 2 A.M.

Los Angeles police, through a program of picking up truants and returning them to school, has sharply reduced crime rates in some areas.

2. ADDED OR SAVED REVENUE   While many cities still use trained policemen for clerical jobs, the Los Angeles Police Department turned over all routine filing and typing to clerk typists, and saved up to $500,000 a year.

Milwaukee has marketed the solids left from its sewage treatment plant as a commercial fertilizer.

The Santa Monica City bus lines make profits, while other municipal bus lines are customarily in the red. Their program: careful advertising, especially attractive bus interiors, special services to the public.

3. FIREFIGHTING   The Chicago Fire Department pioneered a "snorkel" or aerial platform which can thrust as many as five men eighty feet or more into the air, ready to train a nozzle on fires several floors above the ground.

The Los Angeles Fire Department maintains a fire helicopter to reconnoiter remote areas, direct fire-fighting strategy, and perform special services.

4. AIR POLLUTION Los Angeles County, through its own studies and its highly successful control of non-movable air pollution sources, forced both the State of California and the United States government eventually to take action on automobile air pollution.

Pittsburgh has largely solved its smoke problems by well-enforced control regulations and by urban renewal.

5. WATER SUPPLY Denver drove a tunnel through 23 miles of the Continental Divide to bring in adequate water.

Los Angeles, which is currently drawing its water from 350 miles to the east, will soon tap sources 550 miles to its north.

6. MISCELLANEOUS St. Louis submits its crime statistics to regular audit by an independent governmental research institute.

Los Angeles introduced center strip freeway fences and reports that, on some stretches, auto accident deaths have been cut in half.

New York City supports a wide range of treatment centers for drug addicts—including methadone maintenance centers.

Los Angeles employs the usually dry concrete bed of the Los Angeles River to train drivers and to test smog control devices.

Some of these innovations may not prove of lasting importance, but the chief point is that such imaginative experiments are essential if local governments are to remain vital.

Education

Although much of this section deals with administrative innovations similar to those mentioned above, the question of education is so vital that it merits a separate treatment. As we mentioned in Chapter One, earlier slum-dwellers were vastly aided in their upward mobility by the public school system, but there is some evidence that the present residents are not receiving comparable benefits. This situation has been noted by many conscientious educators and there have been serious efforts to improve teaching techniques or to introduce programs particularly geared to specific situations. A good example of the latter can be found in New York City. Certain qualified teachers are sent to Puerto Rico for summer learning sessions in order that they will be better able to understand and to help their Puerto Rican students. John Theobald cites several more generalized efforts made by the same city to give special help to ghetto children.[7] Only one of these, an intensive reading program, seems to be of on-going value. Dr. Kenneth Clark of The City University of New York has prepared a bold scheme with heavy emphasis on basic skills—primarily reading and arithmetic, for the predominantly black students of the District of Columbia. Since it has not yet been put into effect, no evaluation can be made. It would be interesting to know how effective it would be in raising performance among children who are, on the whole, below the national average, because in effect it reverses the modern trend toward diversified and peripheral subjects, and returns to "reading, writing, and arithmetic." In this connection, the experience of one specific Washington elementary school might be cited. Morgan school began an experiment in "community control" in 1967. It was intended to be innovative, and it started out with reading from comic books and with totally undisciplined and totally unstructured classes. Quietly, and apparently with general approval, the early teachers who were enthusiastic advocates of this approach have been replaced by more conventional ones, and discipline, textbooks, and quiet have returned.[8]

Miller and Woock, in their careful study of urban education, review a large number of experiments.[9] Many have proved disappointing. It is sad, for example, to learn that the widely publicized "Head Start" program, of which so much was hoped, has not produced permanent effects. Within a year or two after entering school, the children are doing no better than those who had no preliminary training.

It is a little surprising to discover that black parents frequently have higher aspirations for their children than do the parents of white children in inner-city schools. It is thus doubly depressing when the schools fail to meet the challenge. Miller and Woock cite several studies indicating that low teacher expectations can discourage students. Thus, it is important that teachers especially in ghetto schools should keep high standards and maintain a "positive" atmosphere in the classroom. Studies of this sort should, of course, in turn affect teacher-training methods. The use of teacher aides—drawn from the same community to which the disadvantaged children belong—has sometimes proved of help in keeping the children from feeling that school is a sort of "foreign territory."

That schools in slum districts have difficulty in keeping teachers is understandable. Whereas helping the underprivileged to get a sound basic education may be one of the most worthwhile tasks which could be found, it is certainly not an easy one. It is the writer's personal conviction that good experienced teachers, whether black, brown, or white, should be paid well *above-average* salaries to work and continue to work in ghetto schools. An extra amount of twenty or twenty-five per cent of the regular salary scale is in order, and has ample precedent in the higher remuneration for especially challenging work in industry and in the Armed Forces.

A recent experiment by the University of Wisconsin indicates that children of mentally retarded parents in slum areas can be saved from retardation by special educational services at a very early age.[10] As we have indicated above, not all such programs turn out to be of broad or lasting value, but clearly funds should be available for those which do.

Civic and Business Leadership

One new asset in the attack on municipal problems has recently been noted. Several sociological studies of American communities have discovered a "power structure" quite unlike that which is so widely denigrated—a core of civic and business leaders with a genuine sense of responsibility toward the community. Mayors and managers should actively seek their help on political problems. There is widespread evidence that substantial support can be gained even though these leaders belong to a different political party or do not live in the central city. They are, after all, usually deeply involved in the Central Business District; even though they live in suburbs, they usually introduce themselves elsewhere in the country as "from" the city; they want to be proud of it. They are not remotely interested in the "politics" of seeking local offices. Moreover, from the purely practical standpoint, they are too concerned about their personal reputations to become involved in petty or marginally questionable juggling of interests. American businessmen have their faults, but among the best business leadership there is a great reservoir of unselfish human talent which could be tapped to the advantage of the community. It should be noted that the rebuilding and "clean-up" program of downtown Pittsburgh was carried out by an alliance of Republican business leaders and a Democratic mayor. In the past few years, businessmen in several large cities have greatly increased their efforts to secure employment for hard-core unemployed, especially blacks. It can, of course, be said that not *enough* has been done, but it should also be noted that in the crucial field of jobs, the cooperation of business and industry is indispensable.

Another potential source of support for administrative and political reforms is what might be called the "middle-class idealist." He may, or may not, have any particularly dynamic leadership qualities, but he sincerely wants to improve city government. Here the mayor or the city manager faces the problem of translating vague good will into a functioning force, or of channeling the "one-issue" enthusiast into a group with broader perspective. In New York City, there have been such groups —operating largely within the Democratic party. They have been extremely helpful in ending the Tammany regime. They have not yet been successful in developing a city government responsive to the major needs of reform. But, as we quoted in Chapter Six, New York City may not be too big; it may be too small to do what it is trying to do.

Conclusion

The impatient reader may say: "All this is very well. Boss rule is dying out. Civic and business leadership is turning its concern to municipal affairs. Government officials are attacking their tasks with increased intelligence and imagination. But the *basic* problem of core-city inhabitants is poverty, and that problem has not been solved." The regrettable fact is that the abolition of poverty is not a simple matter. Insofar as poverty is related to employment, the answer to the problem depends upon a wide range of factors: the general state of the economy; the tendency of business and industry to move out from the central cities; and a variety of federal policies. Insofar as poverty is related to cultural problems, the cities could and in the future probably will do more. A concerted effort to enforce housing standards, to expand public health services, to educate police forces to their important function of becoming an understanding and sympathetic agency for promoting cooperation with slum-dwellers, to improve schools, to increase recreational and social services, could have great impact on poverty. Obviously, such a program would take more financing than most cities can now afford; it would require more effective coordination of state, county, and municipal agencies than now exist.

Vitally important to any effective political or administrative action to alleviate the "plight of the cities" is the cooperation of the general citizenry—a somewhat complicated issue to which we shall now turn attention.

URBAN SELF-HELP:
CITIZEN PARTICIPATION

The Problem of Participation

Obviously, *no* government can function without "citizen participation." Autocratic regimes solve the problem quite simply through fear and force. In the United States, we have tried to work through the democratic election process which gives each citizen a voice in the selection of even the highest executive, and through a system of decentralization which encourages each citizen to believe that he can personally affect the governance of his local area. In the past, we have successfully absorbed scores of millions of people from all over the globe and have secured not only their passive acquiescence, but their active cooperation. Our entire system of government rests not only on "the consent of the governed"; it rests on the assumption that "the governed" do not feel "governed." They feel *responsible.* After all, if one householder lets his property deteriorate, the neighborhood suffers. If people do not report to the police crimes within their area, crime will increase. If parents do not encourage their children, public education becomes a farce. If drivers do not observe traffic laws, the entire system of stop signs and intersection lights is meaningless.

It was, therefore, a genuine shock to many Americans to face up to the fact that the riots of the 1960's indicated that thousands of their fellow countrymen had drawn a line between themselves and "The Establishment." While a study of rioters indicated that most were young and single, it also showed that many were employed and were long-time residents of their area. The background of these urban riots is complex, and varying analyses contradict each other. But there is unanimity among all who have studied the riots on one point: the people involved seemed to feel, whether rightly or wrongly, that they could affect various governmental policies only through violent action—not through political participation. The late Professor Oscar Lewis had a theory that there was a "culture of poverty," one of whose features was a disinclination to any kind of organization, voluntary or governmental, on the part of low-income groups.[1] This is an interesting thesis which should not be summarily rejected, but it should be considered in relation to other groups which feel alienated.

A far more affluent class of rioters, a few college and university students, belong to an educational elite which is given opportunities unequalled in 95% of the world. They are rioting against "The Establishment" which has made possible their privileged position. They, too, do not feel that they "belong."

Perhaps one of the most interesting studies of this psychological attitude was made by Herbert J. Gans.[2] It dealt with neither the definitely underprivileged nor with the intellectual radical; it dealt with a group of Italian-Americans living in Boston's former West End who were solid "working class" citizens. They generally believed that politics was corrupt and that the majority of officials were trying to exploit them. They distrusted even those governmental actions which were clearly intended to help them. On the other hand, when urban renewal threatened the continuance of their neighborhood, they could not even organize themselves for effective protest. Their lives were centered in small "peer groups" of similar age and background which discouraged any idea of participating in larger political mechanisms or even in larger coordinated voluntary movements. It is possible that the life of their ancestors in Southern Italy under the autocratic Kingdom of the Two Sicilies and their life in Boston under a political machine dominated by other ethnic groups may have conditioned them against an active interest in participatory democracy. Nevertheless, the fact that these lower middle class people shared with those below them economically and those far above them economically the same sense of alienation from their government, indicates the difficulties to be faced in promoting a sense of participation.

Curiously enough, this wide divergence among the groups who feel "alienated" has received very little attention from either governmental or academic analysts. As we shall indicate in the next section, there are suggestions for local "beautification" projects with no reference to the fact that alienation exists among university students who live on handsome campuses and among slum youngsters who *uproot* the flowers which some people on their streets try to grow. There are projects for "community security" in areas where firemen are stoned for protecting the homes of those who stone. There are projects for interesting parents in local control of schools—when less than 5% can by any means be gotten out to vote on an issue. The writer does not believe that the problem is hopeless; he does believe that something more than organizational gimmicks is essential. The Italian-Americans of Boston's West End kept their apartments clean and tidy and their twelve-year-olds off the street at midnight without any "community project," but they were still indifferent toward municipal government. Gans comments that most of the measures undertaken by the city and by private philanthropy were not what this group wanted or needed. It wanted better employment opportunities and a more effective school system. The approach to these people is not the same approach which might be effective in other groups. It would be well then to realize that the following section deals not with the general problem of alienation, but with a few efforts aimed primarily at slum-area problems.

Methods of Encouraging Participation

The local governments which bear the brunt of the riots and disorders are also the level at which there is the greatest opportunity for working out effective devices for citizen participation. Within the past decade, the federal government, several cities, and many individual students of urban problems have instituted programs or advanced suggestions. This section is largely descriptive. Evaluation will be attempted later.

The Federal government has developed the "Community Action Programs" under the Office of Economic Opportunity and "Model City Programs" under the Department of Housing and

Urban Development. Both of these try to secure the election of representatives of the poor people who will review the community services furnished to their areas by the city with federal aid. Both are clearly intended to encourage the poor to cooperate by giving them a sense of active participation in the programs.

A number of major cities have experimented with various forms of administrative decentralization in the hope that when citizens have a convenient "neighborhood" site where they can ask questions and air complaints, they will have a closer rapport with officials.

Branch municipal facilities—buildings which house staff members of several municipal departments—exist in Los Angeles, San Antonio, and Kansas City. Chicago, Norfolk, and Washington, D.C., have established "Multi-Service Centers." "Neighborhood City Halls" which are, in practice, complaint centers, sometimes with a political overtone, are to be found in Atlanta, Houston, New York, Columbus, Boston, and San Francisco. (The New York projects will be discussed rather fully in Section 3.) Although the particular services rendered may vary from city to city, or even between centers in any one city, the following list is representative of their general nature: counselling, health clinic, day-care center, welfare, vocational rehabilitation, and sometimes special educational programs for the retarded or handicapped.

Almost all of these decentralized programs are paralleled by some kind of independent citizen organizations, but the latter are not usually coordinated in any very clear way with the governmental administrative offices just described.[3]

Individual suggestions for increasing citizen participation, frequently called "community control programs," are numerous. Basic to all of them is the assumption that a sense of participation in the government of a large city is almost impossible—it must be achieved at lower levels.

Unfortunately, some of the suggestions are nebulous. George Schermer writes: "I'm thinking about the creation of neighborhood non-profit corporations, controlled by residents, to manage and maintain property, provide local services, and perform the kind of local security functions that would establish a local code of behavior."[4] There are no details about the formation of such non-profit corporations. Some proposals present constitutional problems. Milton Kotler in his *Neighborhood Government* advocates a neighborhood corporation which would be assigned a share of taxes, would then be independent of the municipal government, would control its own economy, and pass some of its own legislation. It is debatable whether any small area within a metropolis should be so divorced from the whole; it is also legally questionable who would have the right so to re-assign governmental functions.[5]

But there are more thoughtful approaches. Alan Altshuler has written one of the best.[6] He recommends representative neighborhood Councils which would have a veto of city appointments of "field officers" within a neighborhood. District officers would be required to clear with neighborhood Councils. There should be both "agency quotas" and financial inducements to ensure that civil servants live within the district where they serve. The only possible criticism of Altshuler is that he limited himself to the black problem. As we have mentioned before, this is *not* an issue confined to one race.

Another recommendation is summarized by William G. Colman, former Executive Director of the Advisory Commission on Intergovernmental Relations. At the 1970 meeting of the American Political Science Association, he indicated that neighborhood sub-governments should have some clearly delineated boundaries.

1. Where a neighborhood has common concerns and a capacity for local initiative, leadership, and decision-making, all self-help projects should be left to neighborhood Councils, subject only to the reserved right of city, county, state, or federal constitutional authority. Examples of appropriate projects would be supplemental refuse collection, beautification, minor street and sidewalk repair, establishment and maintenance of neighborhood community centers, street fairs and festivals, cultural activities, recreation, and housing rehabilitation.

2. Attention should be paid to population density, population distribution, projected growth, so that a "neighborhood" is not too narrowly defined.

3. The neighborhood councils, which function as the "sub-government," should consist of elected members who either represent a group of blocks, or who are chosen "at large" —depending upon the size and population of the feasible unit. Council members should be remunerated for actual expenses from the resources of the neighborhood, but probably should not be paid for their services.

4. All monies whether from public or private sources should be subject to city, county, and state audit. Authority to raise special levies for these sub-governmental agencies should perhaps be limited.

5. Advisory authority should perhaps be wide in connection with community action programs, urban renewal, public housing, zoning, planning, crime prevention, juvenile delinquency, health, recreation, education, and man-power training.

6. Delegated "substantive authority" is a legal problem which needs careful study both as to extent and procedure.

Do People Participate

Unfortunately, it is too soon to be able to evaluate these new approaches very accurately.

1. It does not seem that either the Community Action Program or the Model City Program has been a spectacular success. Both became enmeshed in politics. The Community Action project faced real difficulty under President Johnson when the organizations of the poor, supported by federal grants, turned against the mayors who were themselves good Democrats and loyal Johnson followers. Therefore, HUD was careful when it set up the Model City system to provide that city governments were to be represented in the local organizations.[7] It was disappointing that CAP elections rarely drew more than 5% of the possible voters, and that the representatives elected did not seem to contribute much.[8] However, both programs are still operating, and are undoubtedly doing some useful work. The point is that they do not seem to have had much significance in arousing a sense of participation among the poor.

2. Since the Association of the Bar of the City of New York has prepared a careful and interesting study of New York's various decentralizing moves (which were, in large part, intended to increase citizen involvement), it is worthwhile to consider in some detail the experience of that one large city.[9]

"Community boards," appointed by the Presidents of each of the five Boroughs, review certain capital projects. Board members tend to be either political followers of the Borough Presidents or already established civic leaders. There is no evidence that this project has measurably increased general citizen interest in government; it certainly has not attracted the poor or disadvantaged citizen.

Under Mayor Lindsay, a number of "neighborhood city halls" have been established. Each is staffed by a half-dozen workers. Chiefly, they function as a referral point for citizens' questions and complaints. This is a useful role, but scarcely a major "break-through." In some cases, there is a "neighborhood cabinet" composed of representatives of the city departments working in the area, who meet to discuss their inter-related services. This, too, is useful, but has no particular impact on citizen participation.

"Urban Action Task Forces" have also been initiated by Mayor Lindsay. A "community secretary" arranges for "community leaders" to meet with a city official to discuss those city-wide problems which affect the smaller community. Here, too, there seems little effect on the basically alienated person.

The Federal government has funded local "community corporations" in some poverty areas. Usually the funds have been allocated to an established social service agency in the area, and usually a very small number of residents bother to vote in elections for members of the corporations.

The Multi-Service Center at Hunts Point, an indisputable poverty pocket, may exemplify one of the hopeful side effects of such an experiment. Aided by federal funds, it has operated a program of local services directed by a locally chosen board. There is no evidence that poorer citizens *on the whole* have been absorbed into a sense of community, but *local* political leaders exist now when there were none before.

Under the Model City Program, New York had three "model neighborhoods": South Bronx, Harlem, and Central Brooklyn. Each of these had a local committee, *selected* by politically experienced local residents. There was apparently considerable confusion about the authority of the city-wide Model City staff vis-a-vis the local committees, and at the time of the Bar Association report, not much had been achieved about spending the $65 million allocated to improve city services in the three areas.

Another New York City experiment in decentralization has received considerable publicity: decentralization in the school system. After the Ford Foundation published the "Bundy Report," favoring decentralization, the New York state legislature in 1970 established the "Community School Boards." These boards are elected from districts; they represent parents and general citizens, and, through a system of proportional representation, do include minority groups. Their situation remains uncertain. To date, the chief issue is the hiring and retention of teachers. Blacks, supported by many liberal sympathizers, wish to exercise control over teachers, many of whom they feel are not adequately or sympathetically trying to educate their children. Teachers unions, dedicated to the thesis of security in tenure, resist any "non-professional" evaluation.

The Bar Association came to the not-very-difficult conclusion that decentralization in New York City is not easy, and that even if it is effectively achieved, no wide-spread citizen participation is guaranteed. The positive note is that some potential leaders among minority groups will be encouraged.

Conclusion

Obviously, many past probings into techniques of securing not only "consent" but "cooperation" from 200,000,000 Americans have not been very successful. As we have indicated, restrictions on innovative ideas may come from state constitutions or from employee unions; from dedicated specialists or from job-conscious bureaucrats; from the disadvantaged themselves who cannot be bothered to participate. As Gans indicated in his study of Italian-Americans, the people in that area wanted jobs far more than they wanted "citizen participation," and they resented the "social worker" approach. Merton also gave several examples of bureaucratic contacts which further alienated the citizen.[10] The New York City experience indicates that, in spite of innumerable projects, the goal has not been even remotely approached. Sometimes, a too "local" orientation may be at cross-purposes with the larger needs of metropolitan planning.

But, just as obviously, the quest for a solution to this difficult problem cannot be abandoned. We are now, for better or for worse, an urban civilization. As we noted in Chapter One, 70% of the population was urban in 1960, and twelve years later the proportion must be considerably higher. Certainly, any decent person would wish to make the average citizen happier but more than individual psychotherapy is involved. The creaking wheel gets the grease partly because the noise is unpleasant but also because the entire mechanism runs better thereafter. It may be that not sufficient attention has been paid to the vastly different types of "alienation." Failure to vote in a school board election is not precisely equivalent to shooting a policeman. It may be that sociology is swamping economics, government, and common sense. The desideratum is a system in which people feel reasonably content to pursue their own life-style under a minimum of governmental control, but with necessary governmental services. Whether through political participation or by other means, a sense of community interest must be stimulated.

THE FUTURE
OF OUR CITIES

9 ★ ★ ★

Franklin Roosevelt initiated the practice of labelling Presidential programs. "The New Deal" became world famous. President Truman sponsored a "Fair Deal." President Kennedy looked toward a "New Frontier." It is interesting that part of President Johnson's "Great Society" included "Creative Federalism" and that President Nixon is working for a "New Federalism." Thus the renewed emphasis on our traditional federal system is strictly non-partisan. It is a practical recognition that in a nation as large and diversified as ours semi-autonomous lower governmental units may be the seed-beds for new ideas and the logical areas for experimentation. In this final chapter, we shall try to assess the roles of the various levels in relation to the most pressing urban problems.

The Federal Government

As we have indicated, a wholesome change in federal attitudes began under President Johnson. It was realized that more than federal grants were necessary to solve the many ills plaguing our cities, and some efforts were made to encourage federal-state-local planning. An Intergovernmental Cooperation Act passed in 1968 eliminated some of the irritating features in earlier grant legislation. The Administration also considered urging some form of revenue-sharing—an idea vigorously publicized by Dr. Walter Heller, Chairman of the Economic Advisory Council. Moreover, the Safe Streets Act of 1965 actually incorporated a "block grant" approach.

The Nixon Administration has gone even further. It has presented to Congress a detailed revenue-sharing plan; it has ordered the collocation of regional offices of a number of national bureaus in order to simplify the work of state and local officials in dealing with these bureaus; it has urged Congress to give the President authority to consolidate separate but closely related grants, subject only to specific Congressional disapproval of any such consolidation; it has worked out a new welfare program which involves closer relations of the federal granting agency with the other levels of government more directly responsible for administration.

All of these are desirable steps, especially the efforts to substitute better methods of sharing revenue than the existing categorical grants. In fact, of course, the role of the national government in connection with urban problems will always be primarily financial, since no other level is so effective a tax collector.

However, there are other useful functions which it could assume. It can raise money for research studies, and it has excellent facilities for collecting information from state and local governments. It can speed up the exchange of ideas throughout the country. The important thing for it to avoid is the viewpoint often held in the past: that Washington must be the sole source of progress in solving urban problems. It is salutary to remember that the state of Wisconsin initiated unemployment compensation and that the county of Los Angeles was long the sole governmental unit seriously working on air pollution control.

There is one type of federal "control" which is clearly proper. Certain minimal standards can reasonably be set. The requirement of no racial discrimination in expenditure of federal funds grows naturally out of the Constitution. Others are within the scope of Congress or federal departments. Accounting to, and some auditing by, federal agencies is a sound policy. Federal funds should not be wasted on uneconomic local units, and therefore it might be wise to continue the requirement that public works projects must be approved by a local planning agency which operates over an entire metropolis. Certain provisions could be designed to encourage cooperation among several local units. The point is not that the Federal government should not set *any* conditions; it is that the conditions should strengthen state and local governments, increase their inter-dependency, not drive wedges into them as do most of the present functional grants.

The State Governments

As we have noted innumerable times, the states, for a variety of reasons, have been the most neglected level of government. Yet in *every* legal sense, and in many legislative, financial, and administrative ways, they are the critical level for attacking the urban crisis. The Federal government should take an active role in changing the old pattern. It should make more grants to the states for the purpose of studying urban problems. It should make it a condition that some grants to states and localities depend upon such studies having been completed. States should be encouraged to become leaders in crime control, to assume full responsibility for all public education, to meet their increasing fiscal obligation to local government, and to use their residual authority to promote local governmental structure better designed geographically and administratively.

States like New York and California will respond with alacrity to such encouragement. They are aware of their problems and are already facing up to them. Other states may move more slowly, but they are far more likely to move with federal leadership than without it.

City Governments

With increased and less fragmented aid from the Federal government, with legal and financial help from the state governments, the task of the city governments will be easier, but still not easy. Mayors and managers need to improve their administrative efficiency; they need to enlist the support of their constituents; they need to "build bridges" with other cities (even at times with other cities which for social or economic reasons their own citizens would prefer to ignore). Cities are the natural place in which to experiment with improved educational techniques, with crime control, and with traffic problems. Leadership from city officials could be very important in prodding state officials into action on the complex anarchy of multiple local governments within a basically unitary metropolitan area. Indeed it may be that intelligent local government could be a decisive factor in a more rational pattern of federal-state-local relations. The writer believes that the recommendation of the Advisory Commission on Intergovernmental Relations is sound: the Federal government to assume the total cost of welfare, the state governments to assume the total cost of public education, the local units to be aided by block grants and/or revenue sharing. The result would be far less urgent financial stress. The need for thoughtful planning of each city's own particular program becomes even more necessary and even more challenging.

The Citizens

Important as state and federal funds are to the solution of many urban questions, *some* degree of citizen interest and participation is absolutely essential. Adequate crime control requires a cooperative public. Any effective approach to the complex of welfare matters must be based on general understanding. Children will gain more from schools if parents stress the values of education.

As we have seen, this problem of citizen participation is not easy. Alienation exists among the affluent youth of suburbs and campuses, among some lower middle class working groups, and among the slum dwellers. While many of the governmentally sponsored attempts to create a sense of belonging are too recent to be properly appraised, the results to date do not seem encouraging. But the fact is that efforts *must* continue. The feeling of "anomie" described earlier may not be entirely eliminated—it is often a personal psychological sort of thing. But there is a broader *community* need to absorb individuals into the realm of governmental interest and activity. There are all too many specific tasks facing us, without adding the handicap of a restless, often inimical, populace. It is true that if the problem of unemployment were solved and if the schools were more successful in both interesting and educating the central city students, some of the explosive potential might be lessened. But education, unemployment, and housing are not easily or quickly coped with, and it is essential that governments which really *are* trying to be helpful secure the patient and sympathetic support of their citizens.

Special Problems

It is certainly true that all four elements viz., the Federal government, the states, municipalities, and citizens, *must* work together. It is also true that, in a rough sort of way, the main importance of the Federal government is financial; the critical contribution of the states is legal and supervisory; the special challenge to municipalities is experimentation and local adaptation; and the responsibility of the citizens is participatory—not inert-cooperation. However, as in all team activities, it may be that in any particular situation or at some particular juncture, one or two team members fill an especially significant function. With these main points in mind, let us review briefly some of the problems we have been discussing.

HOUSING   This is a pre-eminent example of an area in which citizen participation is indispensable. No amount of government planning or government building, whether under federal, state, or local auspices, can make a residential section pleasant if the residents do not try to keep it clean and attractive. The national government is building public housing units at a much higher rate than formerly, but these units often become slums in a disturbingly short time. Some public housing is already abandoned by its tenants. One explanation may be that every slum-dweller hopes to secure a job which will enable him to move to a better section and has no interest in his present neighborhood. Still it must be remembered that there remain desperately poor rural pockets from which inhabitants continue to flee to the cities. Just so long as there is poverty, even without racial overtones of discrimination, there will be a slum problem of some sort and coop-eration of tenants is imperative. Obviously, federal and state money must be available in the first place, and municipal codes must be carefully drafted and firmly enforced.

TRANSPORTATION   Second only to housing as a "physical" problem of the cities is transportation. Downtown traffic conges-tion will probably continue even if, as we grow more affluent, more businesses may move to the suburbs—which already have traffic troubles of their own. A few metropolitan districts may develop rapid transit with federal aid and their own credit re-sources. Federally financed freeways may at least speed up the rush-hour traffic to as much as 40 miles an hour. But it must be remembered that each large city has its own particular environ-mental peculiarities. New York and Boston will certainly con-tinue to rely heavily on rapid transit, and perhaps should ban private autos in central downtown. San Francisco and the entire Bay area will soon be successfully linked by an integrated sys-tem. But it is unimaginable that a city like Los Angeles with its widely dispersed population could ever be satisfactorily served except by private cars. New York has, and undoubtedly will con-tinue to have, its major museums, theatres, etc. on Manhattan Island, but Los Angeles has already embarked on a practically irreversible trend toward decentralization of its attractions. Both resident and tourist must range widely in search of amusement or edification. This problem is primarily "metropolitan" (not municipal in the narrow sense). Even lavish grants of federal or state funds should be subjected to careful scrutiny if they threaten to upset reasonable metropolitan plans.

URBAN AESTHETICS   As our prosperity continues, we may expect some improvement in the general appearance of the cen-tral city. However, this will come through erection of more at-tractive buildings and through planting of expensive sidewalk trees by private owners. The financially troubled local govern-ments can contribute little to such programs in view of other demands. But each city can plan its future development with a combination of realism and imagination and can enforce its physical standards rigorously. Moreover, state governments, it is to be hoped, will establish the local machinery needed for metropolitan planning and action. It is also to be hoped that state and federal governments will respect, in their financial grants, any reasonable over-all plans. We have already noted the lamentable case of federal highways which sometimes run (literally!) at cross purposes with Model Cities.

CRIME AND LAW ENFORCEMENT   Usually considered a "local" concern, this is an area in which federal and state leadership could have real impact. As we have commented earlier, federal-state-local cooperation in the public health field has on the whole produced very good results. Such cooperation has, thus far, been lacking in the field of law enforcement. The Safe Streets Act contained genuinely constructive provisions for meshing federal-state-local programs, but unfortunately it is not typical. No possible "machinery" can eliminate crime, but thoughtful planning could do much to cope with organized crime and to improve policing techniques.

Many of the suggestions which have been prompted by conspicuous weaknesses in "riot control" are applicable on a broader range. We may continue to have riots in crowded city areas, especially on hot summer evenings, by vigorous young males with nothing more interesting to do. But there could be a vast improvement in the training, equipment, and general attitude of city police, and this is a joint responsibility of the Department of Justice, the states, and the municipal authorities. No one denies that policemen can hardly be faulted for reacting somewhat violently when one of their fellow-officers, in pursuit of his legal assignment, is shot in the back for no apparent reason. The important question is: Why does a basically decent slum-dweller feel more sympathy for the homicidal sniper than for the neighborhood policeman? It is this latter attitude which all governmental levels must face and try to change.

Closely related to crime and local law enforcement is a multitude of other factors. The almost incredible slowness of the judicial system is one example. Trials are postponed, literally, for years. Technicalities multiply. Decisions are reversed, and re-reversed. And, after sentence is passed, "correctional institutions" do not "correct"—they often function as effective schools in crime for the first offender.

Certainly, improved health, welfare, employment opportunities, and education (all very broad areas in themselves) will, as the Kerner Report insists, reduce the peripheral incentives to crime. Just as surely, speedy, impartial, and efficient law enforcement will discourage the criminal who is something more than a sociologically disadvantaged waif. This is a very controversial topic, but obviously it involves state and Federal governments as well as the local police.

WELFARE   It may become necessary, as the Advisory Commission on Intergovernmental Relations suggests, to turn all welfare over to the Federal government. It is not desirable that vastly differing standards of subsistence should depend upon an arbitrary state line, nor is it desirable that the poor should surge into a "high-welfare" state simply to capitalize on the differing standards—a trend encouraged by the recent Supreme Court decision against residence requirements. While President Nixon's family assistance plan has much to be said in its favor, this elimination of state differentials is a difficulty. Services in the lowest-welfare states will be upgraded; services in the higher-welfare states (where cost-of-living is usually greater) cannot be maintained without considerable state and local subsidies. And this, again, involves the Supreme Court decision. States might be quite willing to subsidize their *own* poor at a higher rate, but they might reasonably say: Any new federal legislation, under the Supreme Court decision, requires that we treat the 24-hour resident exactly as we treat the 24-year resident. Therefore the differential remains unless we downgrade our own program. The author does not wish to get into undue technicalities but merely to point out that welfare is no longer a matter of "taking care of one's own." It involves executive-legislative-judicial branches of the Federal government, the state governments, the municipal governments.

EDUCATION   Some sociologists think that education will solve all slum problems: educated people will improve their own environment, discourage crime within their own area, and so improve themselves economically that they will move out of the area. Not long ago, two Jewish friends of the author pointed out how much the "Yankee school marms" of the first quarter of the twentieth century had contributed to their absorption into America. But the problem of the inspirational impact of non-Yankee "school marms" of today on the blacks and the Puerto Ricans is somewhat less simple. We shall not wander into such fascinating by-paths as: when all teachers eschew any interest in pay so as to pursue their chosen profession and when all slum-dwellers are so educated as not to be any longer slum-dwellers, what happens? We shall try to address ourselves to present realities. Are the inner-city schools doing a good job? In some cases they are; in some cases they are not. Money is, of course, an important item. If the Advisory Commission's recommendation that states should assume all costs of public education were adopted, many inequitable strains on particular cities would be relieved. Special federal grants to disadvantaged urban areas are undoubtedly justified. But money—from whatever source—is not a guaranteed panacea. Money may aid, but it never created, a good school system. Each area must face its own particular problems and use the money supplied in the way best adjusted to very local situations.

EPILOGUE ★

Clearly many patterns have changed since the central city was both the cultural and economic focus of American life and a major factor in "adjusting" minority groups to their new environment. Such "minorities" as Jews and Orientals who passed through ghettos are now well ahead of the white Anglo-Saxon Protestant element by both financial and educational standards. Most other ethnic groups are firmly and quite comfortably entrenched in Suburbia or in the more desirable neighborhoods of the large cities. Some are and some are not "assimilated" in the simplistic sense of that term, but whether there should remain pockets of Jewish culture, Oriental culture, Slavic culture, or Black culture is a problem quite distinct from the main focus of this booklet. The fact is that true "core city" residents are now predominantly under-privileged blacks, Puerto Ricans, and poor white emigrants from impoverished areas in the United States.

This presents a new challenge. It would be fiscally possible by subsidies from federal, state, and affluent adjacent areas to support the inner cities on a permanent poor-relation basis. Is this what we want? Is it not possible that cities can in the future be what they have been in the past—centers of dynamic new ideas? Charles Abrams has written a book entitled "The City is the Frontier." Although the author does not agree with some of Mr. Abram's suggestions, the title is stimulating. Cities are currently the obvious milieu for major advances in health care, education, welfare plans, law enforcement techniques. Of course, professional research is essential, but even more essential is a change in the thought patterns of all levels of government and a substantially greater participation of the "ordinary citizen" residing both in the inner city and the adjoining areas.

The federal government certainly must rethink, not so much its major policies—which are on the whole well intended—but its techniques. It alone has the decisive financial power to help solve urban problems, and it has *tried*. Currently it is devoting about $30 billion annually to various urban good causes. This money is allocated through hundreds of grants determined by innumerable congressional committees and federal bureaus. Often both the terms of the appropriation acts and the administrative methods prescribed by the bureaus bear little relation to the specific problems of individual cities receiving the money.

Certainly there should be *some* place in the federal government which has clear responsibility to over-see a better planned and better organized channelling of federal money, most properly through state agencies, to the cities. However, the writer does not advocate adding another federal bureau or agency to an already too over-expanded and under-integrated system. The following suggestion seems reasonable.

The Advisory Commission on Intergovernmental Relations has done an excellent job of studying state and local problems, and has made extremely perceptive recommendations to federal, state, and local governments. But it is, after all, an *advisory* commission. Its staff includes some good research specialists, but it lacks politically aggressive individuals comparable to those in many federal agencies who have pushed through their programs. The Kestenbaum Commission, parent of the Advisory Commission, recommended in 1955 that the Executive Office of the President (which includes Budget) assume more administrative responsibility for intergovernmental relations. The Bureau of the Budget has now been renamed the Office of Management and Budget. If the President were to direct that the Office of Management and Budget, so far as is practicable, carry out the recommendations of the Advisory Commission, much might be accomplished. (The reader undoubtedly knows that an executive Department cannot submit to Congress a budget not approved by the Office of Management and Budget. The procedure is complicated, and Congress has many residual powers, but at least the Executive Branch of the Government could accomplish much.)

As we have previously noted, it is all too often forgotten that the states have immense residual constitutional powers over their "creatures"—the cities and counties. If direct federal-urban

relations have often ignored these, the states are themselves frequently to blame. Until recently most of them have not realized
that there *are* serious urban problems and that they could, in
many statutory ways, alleviate them. The role of the states is not
primarily fiscal, but political and legal. The leadership needed
will require aggressive administrators and well informed civil
servants. As has already been noted a few state governments
have already realized that their most serious problems are
largely urban and have set up bureaus of urban affairs. Many
more must do so. These should be staffed with well-trained people who are not only thinking, studying, consulting with experts
but who are also willing and able to work with the legislators
who are broad enough to see the state-wide economic and social
importance of revitalizing the core cities.

The states could, with relatively little expenditure of money,
accomplish much by judicious control of the mechanism of local
government. Although as noted earlier, F.H.A. requirements
have done much to impede the mobility of certain groups, it
would be possible for the states to pass laws which would enable
the blacks and other minorities to move from ghettos to more
livable suburbs whenever they had developed sufficient financial strength to do so. The states alone can do much to solve the
problem of poor city versus rich suburb by legislating "metropolitan areas" which included both. The writer doubts the wisdom of the California Supreme Court's recent decision to use
judicial means to change local school tax policy, but he fully
agrees that there should be state legislative and administrative
steps to help the poor school district do as good a job of education
as does the wealthy school district.

Obviously, local government must have a leading role in any
efforts to solve urban problems. It must be aggressive and informed in using the financial help given it by the federal government and the legal support accorded by improved state policies.
Workable administrative mechanisms, a city council character-
ized by strong leadership, responsible and coordinated municipal units—all are essential.   .

Closely related to the role of the local government in this over-all attack on urban problems is the need for an interested and active civic leadership, including labor and business. No one agency and no one group can solve the social and economic problems facing the core cities. Cooperation from all possible segments is imperative: employers; unions which control access to employment; schools; vocational education agencies; public and private health agencies; local housing, zoning, and building departments—all must work together.

Finally, and this will be the the subject of another book in this series, it will be necessary to arouse in the "ordinary citizens" a sense of participation. Certainly until the core city citizens themselves feel involved in the body politic and display ambition, drive, and responsibility, little can be achieved. It is also essential that suburbanites realize that it is to their own interest (and not merely some vague moral cause) to assist in raising the general tone of the entire metropolitan area.

Clearly we all face a tremendous task. But America in the past has not shrunk from challenges. We arose from the Great Depression to unprecedented prosperity; starting from a state of total unpreparedness we achieved the power to win World War II; after a justifiable determination to defeat decisively the governments with which we were in conflict, we showed both the will and the ability to assist the people of those countries in their efforts at rehabilitation; sending men to the moon is only the most dramatic example of our many miracles of imagination and technology. There is little reason to doubt that we can meet this new challenge to our intelligence, our skills, our drive, and our humanity.

FOOTNOTES
FOR ALL CHAPTERS

1

1 Alan K. Campbell, (ed.) *The States And The Urban Crisis* (1970), p. 15.
2 *Washington Post,* December 20, 1970, Section B, p. 1.
3 James J. Wilson, "Crime" in *Toward A National Urban Policy* (ed.) David P. Moynihan (1970).
4 Edward C. Banfield, *The Unheavenly City* (1970).
5 Advisory Commission on Intergovernmental Relations, *Urban America and the Federal System* (1969), p. 11.
6 *Report of the National Advisory Commission on Civil Disorders* (1968), p. 127.
7 Francis Keppel, "Changing Patterns of Urban Education" in *The Urban Crisis* (1969), pp. 122–123.
8 James S. Coleman, *Equality of Educational Opportunity* (1966).
9 Annie Stein, "Strategies of Failure" in *Harvard Educational Review* (May, 1971), Vol. 41, No. 2, pp. 158–204.
10 John Theobald, "Education" in Lyle C. Fitch and Annamarie Hauch Walsh (ed.), *Agenda For A City* (1970), pp. 165–205.
11 Harry L. Miller and Roger R. Woock, *Social Foundations Of Urban Education* (1970), chs. 8, 9, 10.

2

1 Alan K. Campbell, and Donna E. Shalala, "Problems Unsolved, Solutions Untried" in Alan K. Campbell (ed.), *The States And The Urban Crisis,* p. 12.
2 Advisory Commission on Intergovernmental Relations, *Fiscal Balance In The American Federal System* (1967), Vol. II, Figs. 4–5.
3 Francis Keppel in David McKenna (ed.), *The Urban Crisis* (1969), pp. 12–14.
4 John C. Bollens, *Special District Governments In The United States* (1961), p. 2.
5 *Ibid.,* p. 50.
6 Herbert J. Gans, *The Urban Villagers* (1962), p. 166.
7 "Angry Young Doctors are Rebelling" in *Parade Magazine* (Feb. 21, 1971), pp. 4–5.

8 Leavers, Bernstein, Ranschberg, and Morris, "City Personnel: The Civil Service and Municipal Unions" in Fitch and Walsh (ed.) *Agenda For The City* (1970), p. 621.
9 Herbert J. Gans, *Urban Villagers* (1962), pp. 269 ff.
10 Cited by A. James Reichley in Alan Campbell (ed.), *The States And The Urban Crisis* (1970), p. 178.
11 Alan K. Campbell and Donna E. Shalala, "Problems Unsolved" in Alan Campbell (ed.), *The States And The Urban Crisis* (1970), p. 11.
12 "Problems Unsolved," *Ibid.*, p. 15.

1 All figures are taken from the 1972 Special Analyses Budget of the United States Government, 1971, p. 241.
2 Stephen K. Bailey and Edith E. Mosher, ESEA, *The Office Of Education Administers A Law,* Chapter II (1968).
3 *Ibid.*, pp. 216 ff.
4 Charles Martin Sevilla, *Asphalt Through The Model Cities* (1971).
5 National Urban Coalition, *Law And Order* II (1970), Washington, D.C.
6 ACIR, *Making The Safe Streets Act Work* (1970), Washington, D.C.
7 Report of the President's Task Force, *Model Cities: A Step Towards The New Federalism* (August, 1970).
8 *Ibid.*, p. 10.

5

1 369 Supreme Court 186 (1962); 84 Supreme Court 1362 (1964).
2 A. James Reichley, "The Political Containment of the Cities" in *The States And The Urban Crisis* (1970) p. 173.
3 Thomas R. Dye, "State Legislative Politics" in Jacob and Vine, *Politics In The American State* (1965), ch. V.
4 Advisory Commission on Intergovernmental Relations, *State-Local Finances* (Dec. 1970), p. 15, Table 6.
5 Terry Sanford, *Storm Over The States* (1967), p. 27.
6 *Ibid.*, p. 30.
7 A. James Reichley, "The Political Containment of the Cities" in Alan Campbell (ed.), *The States And The Urban Crisis* (1970), p. 184.
8 The best source is *State Aid To Local Governments.* Advisory Commission on Intergovernmental Relations (1969).
9 John N. Kolesar, "The States and Urban Planning and Development" in Alan Campbell (ed.), *The States And The Urban Crisis* (1970), ch. V.

10 "The State Urban Development Corporation" in *The Urban Lawyer* (Summer, 1969), Vol. I, No. 2.

11 Frank A. Colcord, Jr., "Decision Making and Transportation Policy: A Comparative Analysis" in Bonjean, Clark, and Lineberry, *Community Politics* (1971), p. 276.

12 Advisory Commission on Intergovernmental Relations, *Fiscal Balance In The Federal System* (1967).

13 Advisory Commission on Intergovernmental Relations, *Urban America And The Federal System* (1969).

14 Terry Sanford, *Storm Over The States* (1967), p. 79.

15 *Impact Of Federal Urban Development Programs On Local Government Organization And Planning*, ACIR (1964).

16 Commission on Intergovernmental Relations, *Report To The President* (1955).

17 *State Involvement In Federal-Local Grant Programs*, ACIR (1970), p. 67.

18 Terry Sanford, *Storm Over The States*, p. 170.

1 Advisory Commission on Intergovernmental Relations, *The Commuter And The Municipal Income Tax* (1970).

2 *Ibid.*, p. 97.

3 *The Washington Post* (Dec. 26, 1970), p. 12.

4 David Bernstein, "Financing the City Government" in Robert H. Connery and Demetrios Caraley, *Governing The City* (1969), and Dick Netzer, "The Budgets: Trends and Prospects" in Fitch and Walsh, *Agenda For A City* (1970).

5 *The Washington Post* (March 7, 1971), pp. Bl, B7.

1 Daniel R. Grant, "Urban Needs and State Response" in Alan Campbell (ed.), *The States And The Urban Crisis* (1970), pp. 68–71.

2 International City Managers Association (1970).

3 Arlington County, *Report To The Citizens* (1970).

4 All exact figures cited in this section come from answers to a questionnaire sent out in 1970 by the *Municipal Yearbook*.

5 Robert L. Lineberry and Edmund P. Fowler, "Reformism and Public Policy in American Cities" in Bonjean, Clark, and Lineberry, *Community Politics* (1971), p. 277 ff.

6 Many, but not all, are taken from Gordon, Mitchell, *Sick Cities* (1965).

7 John J. Theobald, "Education" in Fitch and Walsh, *Agenda For A City* (1970).
8 *The Washington Post* (July 6, 1971), Al and A6.
9 Harry L. Miller and Roger R. Woock, *Social Foundations of Urban Education* (1970).
10 Stephen P. Strickland, "Can Slum Children Learn" in *American Education* (July, 1971), Vol. 7, No. 6, pp. 3–7.

1 Oscar Lewis, *La Vida* (1965), Introduction.
2 Herbert J. Gans, *The Urban Villagers* (1962).
3 George J. Washnis, *Little City Halls* (January, 1971).
4 George Schermer, "Urban Social Dilemmas" in David McKenna (ed.), *The Urban Crisis* (1969).
5 Milton Kotler, *Neighborhood Government* (1969).
6 Alan A. Altshuler, *Community Control* (1970).
7 Daniel P. Moynihan, *Maximum Feasible Misunderstanding* (1969). See especially Chapter VII.
8 *Maximum Feasible Misunderstanding,* p. 138.
9 These notes are taken from a discussion draft issued by the Association in late 1970.
10 Robert K. Merton, *Social Theory And Social Structure* (1968), p. 256 ff.

TOPICS FOR PAPER OR ORAL REPORTS based on material and bibliography in the Politics of Government Series

1 Action and Interaction of Interest Groups upon Each Other
2 The Impact of Interest Groups upon Public Opinion
3 The Influence of Invisible Government
4 Means of Communications and Public Opinion
5 Responsibility of Lobbyists
6 Effective Techniques of Lobbyists
7 Advantages of the National Party Convention
8 Influence of Martin Van Buren on the National Nominating Process
9 Success of the National Nominating Conventions
10 Purpose of the National Party Convention
11 Early Experiments in the National Nominating Process
12 Andrew Jackson and the Nominating Process
13 Proposals for Breaking up the Ghettos
14 The Vast Problems of the Central Cities
15 The Feeling of "Anomie" and its Cause
16 The Influence of 19th Century Immigrants on Municipal Government
17 Problems Created by Ethnics and Blacks in the Inner City
18 Home Rule for Large Cities
19 The Effect of Unionization of City Employees on Local Government
20 Responsibility of State Government for the Cities
21 Fiscal Responsibility of State Governments
22 Advantages of the Corporation
23 The Importance of Bigness in Corporate Enterprise
24 The Meaning of Laissez Faire
25 Significance of the Industrial Revolution
26 The Doctrine of Social Responsibility
27 The Split Atom of Property
28 The Policy of Competition
29 Recognition of the Rights of the Consumer
30 The Making of a Successful Lobbyist
31 Effectiveness of the Business Lobby
32 Labor as an Interest Group

BIBLIOGRAPHY ★

Abrams, Charles. *The City Is the Frontier*. New York: Harper Colophon, 1967.

Advisory Commission On Intergovernmental Relations. *Fiscal Balance In The American Federal System*. Vols. I and II. Washington, D.C.: Government Printing Office, 1967.

Advisory Commission On Intergovernmental Relations. *Impact Of Federal Urban Development Programs On Local Government Organization and Planning*. Washington, D.C.: Government Printing Office, 1964.

Advisory Commission On Intergovernmental Relations. *Making The Safe Streets Act Work*. Washington, D.C.:Government Printing Office, 1970.

Advisory Commission On Intergovernmental Relations. *State Aid To Local Governments*. Washington, D.C.:Government Printing Office, 1969.

Advisory Commission On Intergovernmental Relations. *State Involvement In Federal-Local Grant Programs*. Washington, D.C.: Government Printing Office, 1970.

Advisory Commission On Intergovernmental Relations. *State-Local Finances*. Washington, D.C.: Government Printing Office, 1970.

Advisory Commission On Intergovernmental Relations. *The Commuter And The Municipal Income Tax*. Washington, D.C.:Government Printing Office, 1970.

Advisory Commission On Intergovernmental Relations. *Urban America And Federal System*. Washington, D.C.: Government Printing Office, 1969.

Altshuler, Alan A. *Community Control*. New York. Pegasus, 1970.

"Angry Young Doctors Are Rebelling." *Parade Magazine,* Feb. 21, 1971.

Arlington County. *Report To The Citizens*. Arlington, Virginia, 1970.

Association Of The Bar Of The City Of New York. *A Discussion Draft For A Symposium On Decentralizing New York City Government*. New York, 1970.

Bailey, Stephen K. and Mosher, Edith E. *The Office Of Education Administers A Law*. Syracuse. Syracuse University Press, 1968.

Baker v. Carr, 369. Supreme Court Reporter. 186, 1962.

Banfield, Edward C. *The Unheavenly City*. Boston. Little, Brown, and Co, 1968.

Bollens, John C. *Special District Governments In The United States*. Berkeley and Los Angeles. University of California Press, 1961.

Bonjean, Charles M., Clark, Terry N., and Lineberry, Robert L. *Community Politics: A Behavioral Approach*. New York. The Free Press, 1971.

Campbell, Alan K. (Ed.) *The States And The Urban Crisis.* Englewood Cliffs, New Jersey. Prentice Hall, 1970.

Coleman, James S. (and others). *Equality Of Educational Opportunity.* Washington, D.C.:Government Printing Office, 1966.

Connery, Robert H. and Caraley, Demetrios. *Governing The City.* New York. Praeger, 1969.

Fitch, Lyle C. and Walsh, Annamarie Hauch (eds.). *Agenda For A City.* Beverly Hills. Sage, 1970.

Gans, Herbert J. *The Urban Villagers.* New York. Macmillan, 1962.

George, Henry. *Progress And Poverty.* Many Editions.

Gordon, Mitchell. *Sick Cities.* New York. Penguin, 1965.

Grodzins, Morton. *The American System.* Chicago, Rand McNally, 1966.

International City Managers Association. *Municipal Year Book.* Washington, 1970.

Jacob, Herbert and Vines, Kenneth N. (Eds.) *Politics In The American States.* Boston. Little, Brown and Co., 1965.

Kotler, Milton. *Neighborhood Government.* Indianapolis. Bobbs Merrill, 1960.

Lewis, Oscar. *La Vida.* New York. Random House, 1965.

McKenna, David (Ed.). *The Urban Crisis.* Grand Rapids. Zanderman, 1969.

Merton, Robert K. *Social Theory And Social Structure.* New York. The Free Press, 1968.

Miller, Harry L. and Woock, Roger R. *Social Foundations Of Urban Education.* Hinsdale, Illinois. Dryden Press, 1970.

Moynihan, Daniel P. *Maximum Feasible Misunderstanding.* New York. The Free Press, 1969.

Moynihan, Daniel P. (ed.). *Towards A National Urban Policy.* New York. Basic Books, 1970.

National Urban Coalition. *Law And Order II.* Washington, 1970.

Reilly and Schuman. "The State Urban Development Corporation," *The Urban Lawyer.* Vol. I, No. 2. Summer, 1969.

Report Of The National Advisory Commission On Civil Disorders. Washington, D.C.:Government Printing Office, 1968.

Report of the President's Task Force. *Model Cities: A Step Towards The New Federalism.* Washington, D.C.:Government Printing Office, 1970.

Reynolds v. Sims, 84. Supreme Court Reporter. 1362, (1964).

Sanford, Terry. *Storm Over The States.* New York. McGraw-Hill, 1967.

Sevilla, Charles Martin. *Asphalt Through The Model Cities.* Washington, D.C.:George Washington University Urban Law Institute, 1971.

Special Analyses Budget Of The United States Government. Washington, D.C.:Government Printing Office, 1971.

Stein, Annie. "Strategies Of Failure," *Harvard Educational Review.* May, 1971. Vol. 41, No. 2. pp. 158–204.

Strickland, Stephen P. "Can Slum Children Learn," *American Education*. Vol. 7, No. 6. July, 1971.

United States Commission On Intergovernmental Relations. *Report To The President*. Washington, D.C.: Government Printing Office, 1955.

Washnis, George J. *Little City Halls*. Washington. Center For Governmental Studies, 1971.

INDEX ★